THE LAST STRAW: A HANDBOOK OF SOLUTIONS TO SCHOOL BEHAVIOR PROBLEMS

CHRISTINA S. VOLKMANN

San Francisco, California
1978

PUBLISHED BY

R & E RESEARCH ASSOCIATES, INC.
936 INDUSTRIAL AVENUE
PALO ALTO, CALIFORNIA 94303

PUBLISHERS

ROBERT D. REED AND ADAM S. ETEROVICH

Library of Congress Card Catalog Number
77-090364

I.S.B.N.
0-88247-502-9

Illustrated by Esther Rose Graber

TABLE OF CONTENTS

DEDICATION

"TO DON"

INTRODUCTION AND INNOCULATION: FOREWARD

This book is for the day when you want to hang up the chalk forever, for the day when one parent too many didn't like your math program, when the Valentine's Day Party turned into Marat Sade, when the PTA wiretapped your social studies program, when several obstreperous students did several ostentatious things...for the day when even you, yourself, would apply for a job at the local greenhouse because plants don't talk back.

It all has to do with sorting the bumps from the lump---with helping kids to appreciate themselves and others in the confusion of large group interaction. With so many bodies it's hard for a kid to know who and where he is.

Sometimes ideas are short and problems are long for the teacher. If you're teaching in a team situation or are part of a right-on-all-about-it faculty, you have lots of support in problem solving. But sometimes you appreciate the cathartic opportunity to quickly confer with another person's head without ensuing social complications. It's a Gargantuan task making decisions about kids' behaviors all alone in the quiet classroom at 3:30 p.m.; a big responsibility, and you hate to think you're chewing up a child's life without at least checking someone else's ideas. Well, here it is: a head in rectangular, referencial; categorical abstract. I hope it gives you some zany, inspirational ideas or even clues.

This reference book is conceived as an experential resource aid for elementary teachers, designed to investigate many typical classroom problems and their possible solutions. Some of the behavioral areas or problem categories are generalized in order to allow for convenient problem identification. The assignment of sex roles to particular behavioral traits is not literal. This was done merely for convenience and to avoid the overuse of collective nouns and pronouns. Attempts were made to equally delegate female and male characterizations throughout the book.

Hopefully you will find this book before you get to the last straw!

SORTING THE BUMPS FROM THE LUMP

SORTING THE HAYSTACK: PHILOSOPHY OF INVESTIGATING BEHAVIORAL PROBLEMS

Identifying the Teacher Role

In relating to a particular classroom, teachers not only establish a rapport with the students as a whole, but with each individual child. The manner of relating to a problem student soon becomes threefold: It effects the behavior and self-concept of the individual student; it effects the behavior of that student's peers and the classroom ambience; it effects the teaching methods and attitude of the teacher, requiring systematic and thoughtful reflection and reaction. In devising a pervasive solution to a problem, teachers must consider all of the three forementioned aspects. Their actions will effect not only the students with whom they are dealing, but also the remaining classroom. It will also determine the technique in presenting curriculum. Because of these complications, it is often difficult to wisely determine the best teacher role or procedure, or to think of possible alternatives in solving the problem.

What Is the Problem Student?

Students who stand out in the framework of the classroom for whatever reason present problems for the teacher. The individual students are termed "problems" because they require personal responses from the teacher, posing questions of teacher-student strategum. Every student can at sometime be a problem student in regards to the amount of special attention demanded of the teacher, even if for only a short moment during the school day. In normal society, it is quite ordinary to think of responding to each person individually. However, as soon as you place one teacher in charge of 25 to 30 kids, you have destroyed the majority of chances of relating to each individual on a one-to-one basis. Therefore, the "problem" students, as a teacher sees it, are those students who require his personal energy or reactions, drawing attention away from the remainder of the class and creating added burdens for him. The student may not necessarily be socially disruptive; he may

3

merely demand special attention or follow-up by the teacher. It's not that teachers do not enjoy working with students individually or tackling associated difficulties, it's just that an overabundance of such situations is unfeasible. This "problem" exists because there is not adequate time in a teacher's schedule to handle numerous individual causes. Were the student working with a few peers and the teacher, most likely his behavior wouldn't be termed a problem, for the teacher would have adequate time to gratify individual needs. Therefore, when we refer to "problem students," we refer to the many types of students who cause we teachers problems of communication within our classroom structure.

Sensitively devising a precise method of relating to a particular student is necessary to resolve conflicts or to bring out the most positive aspects of the student's personage. All of these constrictures: the individuality of the student (the bumps,) the imposition of the masses (the lump,) and a teacher's effectiveness in dealing with the impersonal structure of education conglomerate to create what we call "the problem student."

In relating to individual students year after year, it seems to be evident that many of the students' more common problems are similar in nature and scope. Is it dangerous to categorize students into problem types? Perhaps. However, there do persist evocative characteristics that are repetitively identifiable among the student population. As mentioned before, students who stand out in the framework of a classroom for whatever reason present problems. Some may even stand out because they are too perfect. Even considering personality variables and idioscyncracies, most problems should fit under basic category descriptions. The danger exists in the tendency to over-simplify the situation and its variables.

There are infinite approaches to the problems presented by students. I will attempt to present a systematic approach in solving these problems, as well as a choice of feasible alternatives in dealing with the student, considering not only the effects on the student, but the effects on the entire class as well as the curricular side-effects.

4

Basic Solution for Problems: DO SOMETHING

Before a problem, what is it? Just a series of events that bug you. Finally they become so frequent that you figure there is a problem in the vicinity. Before a problem can be solved, the hardest part is becoming aware of its existence at the appropriate time. The ability to recognize the potential problem when it is still young is a time-honored and semi-instinctive trait among teachers. Many neophyte teachers experience painful conflicts in classroom control merely because they are not able to recognize soon enough the early signs of trouble. This

DEVISING A SOLUTION

causes dreadful scenes of upset before the problem is identified or defined. The best help in identifying potential problems early is previous experience in your own classroom. For those without this aid, it is wise to tighten your reactions; respond to a situation immediately with a strong affirmative plan, rather than let situations slip by.

Once it is evident that there is a problem with a student, it is best to tackle it immediately. First you need to decide exactly what is the problem behavior. Observe closely several situations when the problem occurs. Note the circumstances that seem to bring on the problem, and the consequences of the situation. If possible, confer with any other person who has worked with the student recently in similar predicaments. Such a person might be his former teacher(s), a counselor, or administrators. Specifically seek information about past behaviors in comparison with present behaviors. Are these new problems? Is the present trend better or worse for the student? Sometimes it is helpful to find out how other people have dealt with the same problems and what they feel was the outcome of their efforts. Take into consideration that due to personality factor nuances, another educator's method of relating to a student may not be the best for you. Each teacher has his own aura with a student, and it may not be comfortable for you to handle the student's problem in the same manner as have prior instructors. When you think that you have the problem defined, mentally explore as many alternatives of action as possible before pursuing your own direction.

Penalty Prevention

The classic penalty in elementary education carries a highly negative and punitive connotation. Penalties have typically been used to control a student by threatening him with unpleasant alternatives. Penalties may still serve this function in today's classroom, but they may also be skillfully designed to impart a positive experience in individual growth. A penalty acts as an actual learning situation rather than merely as a negative behavioral straightjacket. Learning

6

penalties, even when they sometimes could be interpreted as a punishment, offer positive consequences to a disobedient or irresponsible action. Teachers today still impose "consequences" upon their students, whether they be labeled penalties or punishments. Sometimes after trying all other possible alternatives and penalty preventions, teachers resort to penalizing an undesireable behavior; this may or may not bring about the desireable behavior. Reinforcing a desireable behavior is more advantageous than punishing an undesireable behavior, however some learning penalties may need to be imposed when prevention has not sufficed. Once you have defined a certain problem and assiduously begun your course of action, you may feel the need to impose a penalty. Each problem could necessitate a different penalty form, and for this reason the appropriate penalty is not always easily devised.

This book will suggest many learning penalties under the appropriate chapters, but foremost, it will emphasize the importance of penalty prevention. What is meant by penalty prevention? When you're really ill you visit the doctor and receive the appropriate medicine. The rest of the time, you attempt to treat your body well in order to prevent disease. Similarly, penalties may need to be imposed in an elementary classroom when a situation is already deteriorated to a certain degree. Otherwise, you exert much effort to maintain a classroom environment where penalties are not often needed as a treatment. Because the prevention of penalties are not often needed as a treatment. Because the prevention of penalties is so vital to a positive, vibrant classroom, it is in this philosophical portion that specific examples will be revealed. Principles such as these should be the foundation of solving classroom problems; it's only when the foundation seems unstable that you should "patch up" with other penalty forms.

One possible aid in penalty prevention could stem from the activity level of your classroom. By this I mean that if you have special things happening at frequent intervals in your classroom, they can be used for leverage. Some examples? Depending on the interests of the class...one group of my students adored cooking. Every few weeks we would decide something to make: stew, ice cream, carmel apples, gingerbreadmen, bread...sometimes it fit in with another curricular area and sometimes it didn't. It didn't matter if it was vastly educational, because the kids loved it so much that all their other work was affected and greatly improved by the honor of getting to do something genuinely stimulating for a spell. We usually had a few extra things to do concerning the event, such as doubling or tripling the recipe, demonstrating correct measuring procedures, looking up the origin of spices, being responsible for remembering to bring ingredients. Such joy and enthusiasm was manifested during these times (oh no, Jim forgot to bring the eggs!) that they would do anything to retain their participation privileges. Yet we had an understanding that anyone who was raising havoc on or around the big day would lose the right to participate; it was too much hassle having one weirdo spoil the soup. The kids understood the necessity of good behavior as a prerequisite for cutting elementary school bureaucratic red tape: such obstacles as scheduling kitchen time, extra smiling at the custodian to procure his good graces and added inconvenience to his schedule, immaculate cleaning up, not disturbing other classes. All of these provided goals for a unified bunch of workers, and the kids were quick to squelch undisciplined peers for fear of losing privileges.

Another penalty prevention technique was a program of mini student trips where parents would whisk away five different students each week to various secret, forbidden places--like private planes, Japanese gardens, construction sites, open air markets. It was common knowledge that any student who came to school out of sorts or without all assignments completed for the mini trip day would not be allowed to go. Once this occasion occurred to two unprepared students, one of them being the son of the parent who was sponsoring the trip! I was in a quandary over whom to have angry with me: the parent, the kid, or myself for giving in and setting an unstable precedent. As it turned out, I went to the class, telling them that two students weren't eligible and asking them what to do. They discussed it, and voted. The outcome was that they felt both students should have a second chance since it was the first time this had happened. The class said that if the students could have their

8

assignments completed by the end of morning recess, that they should go; otherwise
not. Quite fair. As it ended, the sponsor's son finished, but the other child (a
typical sneak/lazy one) could not terminate because he had too much to do. Letting
the class decide had been ingenious, for now the irresponsible student could only
direct his anger at his peers. Furthermore, as a result of this group decision all

students realized that in order to do fun things, they had to be responsible to themselves and their peers (not to the teacher) both behaviorwise and academically in their daily doings.

By having fun "extra" activities offered every few weeks (others could be tiedyeing, banquets, kite flying and building, frizbee contests, helium balloon experiments, pet days) the kids really are excited about school, and have a greater incentive to contribute positively to class goals and to their education. Without tons of upcoming excitement, there is little value in a deadnosed teacher-imposed penalty.

Finally, this philosophy of behavioral problem investigation is based upon a secure identity of teacher role: the actions of a teacher effect all members of a classroom and the content of the curriculum. As teachers define a problem and choose a solution, they must keep in mind the overall effects of their role in the classroom.

SETTING THE FOUNDATION TO BEHAVIOR PATTERNS

In establishing desired behavior patterns within a classroom, teachers attempt to build certain foundations upon which they rest their course of actions. Three individual areas stand out in my own classroom behavioral foundation: daily class meetings or extrapolations, the physical arrangement of the classroom, and my public relations and parent feedback investment. These three areas, each specific and seemingly isolated in scope, all reflect strongly upon the behavior of my students, and are inherent in my overall educational emphases. Their inter-relation with distinct problem solving is ecclectic.

Extrapolations and Daily Class Meetings

The affective movement in elementary classrooms has been in full swing since the late '60's. Such educational sages as Glasser, Rogers, and Palomares have published many influential and helpful guidelines for opening the paths to meaningful communication and self-awareness in elementary classrooms. Today there are numerous kits and new confluent materials to aid the teacher in mental health education, value definition, and affective education.

Which affective label you choose or whose doctrine you espouse is not gravely important. It is important, however, that you develop some sort of daily method of communicating informally and openly with your students. "Informal" in this sense does not mean lacking in structure, but the chance for both kids and teacher to speak sincerely and without fear of criticism. It is a natural need for each student to feel an integral part of the classroom foundation no matter what his other academic or social conflicts; a daily situation where all class members are structured to act socially and intellectually on a par gives this outlet to each student.

When is it best to have your daily communication session? Some teachers prefer using the final 45 minutes of the day for this chat. For me, early morning is best. At this time pressing concerns can be brought forward especially those which may have benefitted by a night of cogitation before introducing them to the class. When we meet habitually in the early morning, the kids know exactly how we'll start each day and are already in a circle for discussion when the bell rings. This daily time will not be inadvertently drowned out by last minute schedule changes in the itinerary, nor is it overtoned with the tired emotions of a busy day in full swing. Being the first activity, it can be either shortened or extended depending upon the needs of the class. If necessary, additional meetings may be held as problems arise or the need for consultation is evident.

What should this time period be called? If you are prescribing to a strict program such as Magic Circle, Values, TAD kits or you name it, then you will perhaps go by their suggestions. I have always called our group "Extrapolations" which encompasses the flavor I like.

How can a communication group such as this be used? There are thousands of possibilities. Most commonly we discuss "daily doings" and what's going on before delving into heavier areas. Kids feel free to bring up their pervasive concerns spontaneously. We also participate in activities to develop decision making and explore group roles. Role playing is one technique used often to provide awareness about a particular subject area. There are several excellent books published which provide the background and stimulus needed for role playing; teachers who feel deficient in this area should consult the guidance counselor about procuring a book that will direct them in role playing techniques. We discuss our values, our intraclass problems, hypothetical situations, and maybe even plan a Halloween party. This group is used for all sorts of things, social, political, and interpersonal, depending upon the needs of the class as I see them or upon the whims of the kids themselves. As we progress through the year, the group becomes more independent in choosing interesting areas of discussion and is able to pursue a stimulating subject almost without aid of the teacher. I find my role vascillating between that of a controller and that of a defogger. Sometimes I must eyebrow someone or lead a group more than I wish, and othertimes I feel the need to press certain questions when an aspect is being overlooked or distorted.

Each teacher must decide for himself what kind of daily outlet he will establish for group interaction. This outlet is a foundation to behavior patterns because it teaches the kids to converse and to work through problems as a unit. They are continually practicing these skills, and are not abnormally disturbed when a problem subject is introduced because they are accustomed to such discussions. Having developed their skills each day, you may grow to rely upon their judgement in handling disturbances. They realize at the same time that they, as much as you, direct and guide the tone of the classroom, and will rally to aid you in your upsets. A striking example of this type of involvement occurred once when the house of one boy in my class burned down. The boy had not come to school the next day, but the whole classroom was buzzing with the news that "Matthew's house burned down," and that subject was foremost on every child's mind. At extrapolations the story was told by his nearest neighbors. This led to the dilemma: "What should we say to Matthew when he comes back to school?" Everyone gave their views, putting themselves in Matthew's place. It was finally decided by vote that whenever Matthew came back, nothing would be said by anyone except one boy in the class who was felt to be closest to Matthew. That boy (Mike) would be the class spokesman, and would be allowed to ask Matthew if he wanted to talk about it. Later that morning during math, Matthew came to class. He hardly said anything to me---just put a note excusing his tardiness on my desk and hurried to his seat in a waft of stale burnt-house smelling clothes. The class was so silent. No one was outwardly watching Matthew, but everyone was glimpsing him from behind their math problems to the utmost possible. Casually, Mike ambled over and whispered for a few seconds with Matthew. Then he went back and sat down. A good thirty seconds passed when suddenly Mike's voice boomed out, "Matthew doesn't want to talk about it." And that was that. It wasn't until the whole next day that Mike negotiated with Matthew to talk with us at extrapolations about his experience. Matthew had thought it was too embarrassing to talk about, just as the class predicted. Hopefully he was spared a day of social agony and premature invasion of his privacy by the gentle empathy of his classmates. This experience, to me, was a decisive reinforcement of my beliefs in the spiritual support offered by a class group in communication, and served as another component in the foundation of that class' behavior pattern.

Physical Arrangements of the Classroom

The physical layout of a classroom exerts crucial perameters to the overall atmosphere, types of learning activities, and flow of student interaction. The locale where the students are seated or situated within the classroom is a significant component to the amount of intercommunication that will take place, and a pillar in the foundation of behavior patterns.

Every teacher has personal preferences in class arrangements. Most often these preferences will be coupled with the general disposition of the students in the classroom to achieve the total personality of the final arrangement. I always like having a good 1/3 to 1/2 of my floorspace empty to accommodate class meetings, creative drama, informal discussions on the floor, and to create a general area in which to move about. This usually means that the remaining floor area is totally swamped with desks which are very close together. Most of the interesting things seem to happen in the open area of my classroom, and the kids huddle back to their desks for seat work or individual activities. The discomfort of close desk quarters doesn't seem to bother the kids because they like to consult often with their neighbors and spend only minute portions of the day as captives in that area.

In most cases my classes are required to accept my room structure (1/2 open, 1/2 desks) as a basis for organization because that's the way I feel that I teach best, but we usually work together to decide composition of the desk portion within the prescribed area. Sometimes we do zany changes just for the sake of change. Usually the kids are content to regroup themselves into twos, threes, and fours. Some classes have even tried not having any certain assigned desks, but moving desk contents about in trays to allow for mass freedom each day. This,

14

however, is too impersonal for kids; they seem to prefer having the security of a home base and a private domain.

The actual process of moving desks can be tedious and noisy. Sometimes we move all the desks into a suitable arrangement, then the kids fill them as they would like. Othertimes we move everything around within the defined area for fifteen minutes, then stop to see what kind of traffic patterns we have developed among the desks. If something seems too lopsided or impractical, we make new adjustments.

Mandatorily assigning seat positions is autocratic, but sometimes necessary. Some classes do not choose seat partners wisely, or have too many personality conflicts to allow open choices. This situation, fortunately, is not too often the case. Other situations when seats may need to be assigned by the teacher are those instances where two or three kids seem unable to function among other students. A warning should be given to students who are malfunctioning in their location. Then after a period of time, the teacher may be obligated to tell the students that their seats will now be moved to thus and such until their behavior demonstrates that they are able to be more responsible for their actions during the day.

There are many possibilities in class seating organization. But given the classic room arrangement of stationary windows, ventillator, shelves, and chalkboard, there are not often many alternatives for rearrangement. Kids like change as much as you do, and will enjoy the social processes of redesigning their environment. A great way to break the tedium of time as well as stimulate new decision making and social intercourse is to simply change the desk arrangement. Moving desks can also solve peer problems without your personal intervention if the class decides that everyone must seek new seating partners rather than sticking to their own regular buddies.

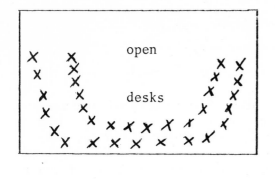

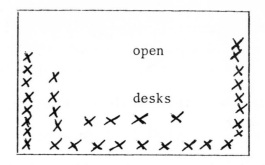

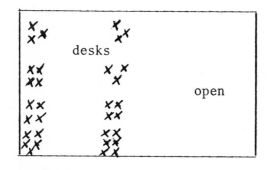

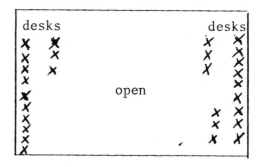

PUBLIC RELATIONS AND PARENT INVESTMENT

OR

PARENTS EYE TO EYE

Parents, like kids, come in infinite varieties. Most parents are extremely concerned about their child's education, and want to see evidence of positive academic and social growth. Because parents are so caring about their children, they will become involved in your classroom by letting you know how they feel about their child's progress under your guidance. The majority of parents will relate their concerns and desires to you in a mature, sincere manner. Other parents who are less sensitive may cause you to grope for more effective methods of communication.

It would seem as though a prerequisite for being a dissident parent of an elementary school aged youngster is a two week course in guerilla maneuvers at a John Birch Retreat or the SLA farmhouse in Pennsylvania. This would entitle them to periodically infiltrate their child's classroom and effectively demand certain procedures of the teacher. If the teacher seemed the least bit subversive, experimental, leftist, or didn't lead the Pledge of Allegiance each day immediately after milk count, then they would have adequate preparation to systematically challenge and destroy the individuality of that teacher. It's a wonderfully powerful feeling for these parents, levying demands for their child's educational welfare.

As a teacher, sometimes it seems every parent is against whatever you're for. Realistically, this isn't true. However, each year there are those parents who don't see eye to eye with you, and you spend countless hours of worrying, negotiating, and being frustrated. These parents seem to drop in at the least expected times (just when you thought everything was going so perfectly,) are always armed fiercely with many acidulous emotional accusations, and usually are philosophically alien to your most milk toast wave length. They usually do not come in only to give you a hard time, but because they love their child very much and feel that she/he is not receiving the attention or educational climate they expect of their school

17

system.

At the other pole there are the parents who manifest in glittered sunbeams, are individually concerned, who offer constructive and helpful criticisms, or drop by merely to uplift your most downtrodden hopes for the year. These parents help you to realize that one of the reasons you're knocking yourself out each year is to nurture more fine human beings such as themselves, people capable of rational communication. Parents to whom you relate successfully are in essence no more concerned about their children than are parents to whom you have difficulties relating. All of them are representing the best interests for their child according to their value system, and are merely expressing to you their satisfaction or dissatisfaction with the opportunities that you offer their child.

There are multitudes of tiny little things a teacher can do to maintain a positive, even-keel rapport with the public and most parents in general. Some of them are a PAIN, but in the long run, the investment will dispell many future periods of deep trouble. Because of the heavy involvement of parents in the behavior patterns of your classroom, working with them is a vital step and a rewarding step in setting your basic foundation. Following are some suggestions:

1)   Orientation

Every September in every elementary school in every classroom there is some form of "Let's Scope Out the Kid's Teach" Night. This is the night when you drag out the dusty electric rollers and curl your hair, and wonder if midi, maxi, mini, or pants would best serve to meet the approval of the masses. Some teachers dread this night and prepare dull, boring talks. Others are afraid of being cornered (it happens everytime) by some frenzied parents who want you to know all of Bobby's past educational history while you're still trying to remember exactly which kid is Bobby---school has only been in session seven days now. There are many demanding social pressures, and you feel under scrutinizing inspection by all parents. The smart teacher prepared mightily for this night and uses it as a spring board for future parent/teacher relations. If a truly personal and meaningful communication is established with your parents on this night, it will result in a warm, unified start for the school year. I suggest three basic areas to be covered during this meeting: Personal Sketch, Educational Philosophy, and Expected Curriculum.

Why give parents insight into your personal life? You needn't tell them what you did last Saturday night, but they are curious about you, and once you open up a bit to them about your educational background and interests outside the classroom, they may (or may not) identify with some aspect of you. Already they will feel you are more of an individual, able to relate to their kid as a human, and may perhaps be supportive of one or two things you have done. They may be shocked that you are not trying to put up a "heap big educator" front, hide your true identity, or be some intriguing closet case that was restored just in time for fall classes. This personal introduction will be invaluable in future parent/teacher conflicts because it is a lot harder to attack someone who has been open and congenial with you than it is to attack Mystery Teacher Number Four. Meeting parents on the level in this friendly, personal fashion is a pleasant and natural way of saying, "I hope we can work together with your child as friends this year."

The Educational Philosophy portion can be a bit tricky. As teachers we are striving to be recognized as professional. Here is certainly a chance to develop and upgrade that image. Don't hesitate to use educational terms and to sound knowledgeable in your field. It's high time that teaching is discussed and exposed as the intellectual and stimulating profession that it is. As you do this you want to give a strong idea of your classroom personality and your gut feelings, but you do not want to alienate parents or leave the field open for violent, controversial debate. I find it best to dwell on how I perceive kids in general, and my hopes for the development of this particular class as human beings. Some examples of more affective learning situations can be used here, such as class meetings or decision making. Emphasis could be made on perameters for decision making and how you hope to guide your students in this process. At this point, a few basic policies or

19

rules could or should be presented--the same policies that the kids have developed for class routine: for example only doctor's excuses will excuse a child from P.E., absentee procedures, fieldtrip policies, lunch business, whether gum may or may not be chewed, your expectations concerning daily work, and your procedures when Junior is not working up to level. In this section it is best not to make too many bold promises or threats. But do provide a basic structure or feeling about your classroom psyche and mechanics. Even the most open or free classrooms thrive on a

structure or principle of operation; let yours be known.

The Expected Curriculum could be as detailed as you like. Show texts and basically outline concepts to be introduced during the year. Any new program that you anticipate being slightly controversial could be supported at this point. If you individualize in any subject areas, your projected pattern of skill development could be presented. Parents are usually satisfied with very general concept introductions, and can easily be kept up with the new areas of study via monthly letters.

A question and answer session is helpful for bringing up points you left out.

Having something extremely creative or eyecatching around that each student has made is a positive stimulus. Lots of times the kids draw and color in a life size cut-out of themselves. Parents enjoy trying to recognize their own kids among the thirty leaping giants taped up all over the room.

2)   Monthly Letters

At the end of every month, four kids write a dittoed letter to all parents telling everything we've done during that month. Four different kids are chosen each time, regardless of performance level. Somehow they each seem to find a positive role in the creation of the letter, delegating responsibilities among themselves according to their abilities and interests. They usually divide it into curricular areas. Commentaries are included, such as, "We all thought this was really fun," or the contrary. At the end I sometimes would write a paragraph or two mentioning upcoming studies or other information that parents should have received. This letter is usually written on Thursday by the four kids, corrected by myself and them, then recopied on dittos by them for distribution the next day. They always personally sign the letters and are proud of their work. The amount of correcting done together is fairly stringent; we work hard to send home a quality letter that not only shows the class' quotidian development, but grasp of skills in communication. Not all work in class needs correction to this degree, but when it involves public relations

21

we like to cast a favorable image. Always mentioned in the letter are the names of the parents who have visited the classroom during that month. This is a psychological hors d'oeuvre for the parents who are anticipating an invitation in the months to come (see Class Visitations, page 23). Parents appreciate hearing what we have done because many students don't talk much about school at home, especially about the emphases in curricular disciplines, and through this medium more parents feel informed about their child's class.

3)   Friday Folders

One particular year many parents complained of never seeing "corrected" papers. Thus was inspired a system whereby each Friday every kid had to take home a folder of all her work from that week, have it initialed by Mom or Dad, and return it on Monday. This was a true drag for both me and the kids, but alleviated those aches and blues of the Forgotten Parents Association. Fortunately this form of public relations was necessary only during that particular year for the specific needs of that class.

4)   Phone Phenomenea

Use the phone for quick conversations about kids--if you're noticing a trend, call the parent before it gets sticky. Have the parent check back via note or phone in a few days if follow-up is needed. Or even call to tell a parent something great their kid did. It does wonders for your P.R. department.

5)   Parent Aides

Some parents don't mind and even thrive on correcting spelling tests, math quizzes, or better yet coming in once a week to work with a few students. This program takes lots of reinforcement and positive feedback on your part to let parents know they are appreciated. I like to use parents for math quizzes because that way I can give one 5-question quiz weekly to check progress without getting bogged down on correcting and recording. Allowing parents to help in class lets them see how lots of varied students complete work, and also exposes them to 1/1000 the amount of paper work and kids' questions digested by teachers daily. Some parents acquire great empathy.

How do you set up a program to involve parents or lay aids? The best way is to send home a letter describing various possibilities for parents to become involved with the class. Also explain why you enjoy having parents in the classroom, and how it helps the kids. At the close of the letter, list discipline areas and specific tasks under each area (for example "MATH: teaching a small group, tutoring a slow student, tutoring an advanced student, correcting papers weekly, correcting papers bi-weekly (indicating at home or at school), and other suggestions as proposed by volunteers." When you suggest concrete areas for participation, parents feel more secure in their commitments. Include a box-in section for time preference, indicating which day(s) of the week they would be available and during what hours. After you have tabulated all the results, you can decide how best to use your volunteers. Let them know when you'll begin to use them by sending a note or by a phone call. From this point on most of your contacts will be with parents on the individual basis, but when you have two or more who are directly involved with teaching, it is strongly advised to schedule a couple of short informal workshops to give them teaching hints and to let them encourage one another. Be sure to have the parents commit themselves only for one semester or trimester, then reorganize. This way they can terminate their work at an anticipated date if dissatisfied. It's easy to lapse into slipshod scheduling, leaving parents dangling or insecure as to their responsibilities. Their esteemed help is too valuable to squander or to leave unacknowledged. A neat way to thank parent helpers is to throw a tea or a general coffee hour some night after school.

6)   Class Visitations

I love class visitations. Three sets of parents are invited to come on a certain day anytime from 9:00 a.m. to 12:00 a.m. By issuing invitations at least two weeks ahead, many working parents can arrange to get away for an hour or two. The child writes the invitation "to come visit" him and his class, and is responsible for letting me know if his parent is coming or not so that replacements can be found. Parents are told to please come on in, sit down, and make themselves at home. Some kids like their parents to join them at their desk while others remain comically aloof. No giant deal with introductions is made; life continues on, and if it seems to flow, then the parent may become involved in what we're doing. Sometimes the visitors give spelling words or listen to readers. Others prefer to be left in peace and free to roam. I generally try to choose visitation times when there is a good portion of academics, at least reading or language arts and math, otherwise parents are freaked it they happen to come the day we have P.E., music, then baking. Mornings are the best time in my experience as the kids are more fresh and vigorous. One thing: encourage parents to stay at least one hour. Just drifting in for one moment doesn't offer a reliable impression of the total concept presentation. Also, by remaining a longer period of time, parents are apt to see at least two curricular areas, and hopefully two very different methods of instruction...for example math may be quite structured or cognitive (not necessarily!) and the following language arts class may be extremely creative and active. Many parents who were skeptical of their child's destiny in my classroom express a grand reversal after their visit. I fervently try to schedule those anxious-looking parents early in the year, so that they have less time to sit at home and stew about the unknown subversion befalling their little darlings. It's desirous to at least get in a sentence or two with the parents when they come, but sometimes with all the distractions and submersions, it's almost impossible. At least a warm smile and wave across the room lets them know you're glad they could come.

7)   Friday Notes

Friday notes are another quicky way to keep in touch. Refer to the chapter on Zero Self-Concept, page 75, bolster notes.

Most schools have room mothers. Room mothers always seem to be involved
in the underground some way or another. One year my team partner and I had four
room mothers, two of whom transferred their little gems from our subversive program
before Christmas, and the other two who campaigned against us for the major part of
the year. Not all room mothers are that fatal. I usually wonder what to do with
them. They're always lurking out there somewhere with their shiny spatulas waiting
to frost another cupcake whereas the kids actually chose grape soda and red licorice
as their refreshments. Then they bring in their out-of-control games for Valentine's
Day and you spend 3/4 of the party time peeling spaced-out kids off the walls. So
I usually tell my room mothers in September that I don't use room mothers too much
for parties because kids like to plan and execute (literally) their own parties, but
that I will try to use them as often as possible for other special occasions. (When
are those?) Room mothers still baffle me.

9)   Beetlejuice Smashers

It is difficult to work with some parents no matter what you try. You
have to see their point--if they don't like the way you run the class, they are not
going to be able to idly stand by while you corrupt their kid. In this extreme case
it is better to transfer the kid early in the year (the principal hopefully should
have prevented these gross situations by his class placement if he were aware of
personality clashes). If this is not possible, try to find one platitude of peace to
reconcile your differences and work from there.

Youngsters come to school in infinite variety of personality and character. No matter how you generalize their basic traits, each one is a unique individual who offers a fresh outlook to behavior patterns and life situations. In categorizing various student types, it is necessary to remember that kids will not be readily fitted to one certain stereotype. The similarity of a child's actions to a descriptive label may be minimal. Much the same, the treatment you devise for each child will vary according to the differences in character. A child cannot merely be plugged into a certain procedure. Each behavior situation demands a specific evaluation by the teacher in order to deal with a problem (see pages 3 through 6, Sorting the Haystack). In referring to the generalized student descriptions and possible solutions in this portion of the book, teachers should carefully evaluate and readapt the material therein to the subtle diversities of their own teaching situations.

Some educators may feel distraught at actually seeing in print the same casual references they make daily toward students. All teachers talk about their bullies, sneaks, and thieves, but somehow the educational textbooks have never admitted they exist in print. In identifying and labeling such negative types of behaviors, we are not attempting to demean or belittle a student; these terms are used because they best describe a student type, unpleasant as she/he may be, and because these terms are universally used among active teachers in characterizing students. The labels are not meant to be simplistic or as put-downs for kids, but merely as concrete, teacher-utilized descriptive handles.

The Bully

This whole category has to do with Big Fistness, Organized Grime, and Recess-ion. Big Bully has the physical advantage of always having had Space Sticks for breakfast. Furthermore he has the political conscience of a Nixon aide and the mental prowess of an ICBM. The obstreperous bully, whose parents and relatives are all under 5'2", knows his time is limited and is making up for future days when he'll be sentenced to platform shoes. Elementary school is the "now" for the bully, and his karma is known for six blocks around.

It is normal that some students will intimidate others by their physical size, guts, superior coordination, or verbal domination. This characteristic is not a problem until it becomes destructive, aggressive, or overly-exercised.

Possible Solutions

When it is evident that a certain student is bullying too often, some of the following suggestions may be helpful:

1) Confer with the bully privately. The first meeting should be non-threatening. You might observe several situations, then discuss them with the bully. Tell him what you saw. Ask him, "How were your actions helping you? Can you think of anything else you could have done in that situation?" Tell the bully that you will be observing him, and will let him know immediately the next time you see him bullying or dominating. The bully will always have a perfectly logical excuse for why he was behaving in such a manner, and oftentimes is not even aware that the actions are necessarily bullyish to others. For this reason, it is usually necessary to tell him when he is in the process of bullying.

2) If next time occurs, it is essential to stop what you are doing immediately and say to bully, "Bully, may I talk with you at...(state an exact time)?" Review at that time with bully exactly what happened, letting him do the talking. Ask him to give his ideas of what the situation involved. Then negotiate what might have been a better conduct and set up an agreement whereby you can signal bully easily in the future when he should change his behavior. I have tried such clever moves as "touching my thumb to my ear" with bullies who not only had a physical dominance problem, but also tried to dominate oral situations; they lacked discretion in determining an appropriate length of speaking time. One boy was truly unable to judge and control his verbosity or his temper. After several unsuccessful attempts to leave these decisions up to the bully, he and I decided that he would like me to help him.

We elected to try the ear signal. For some strange reason, he was very happy to have me perform my tricky signal during group discussions or games and would stop talking or pushing as soon as he saw me touch my ear. No one else in the class knew of this arrangement, and this bully was proud of his secret pact. He seemed to need the private recognition, or perhaps wanted someone to control him, just as he had the need to control others.

As far as physical violence goes, the bully must be penalized when he is

aggressive in this way. This violence should not be tolerated after the bully has been counselled once. Because pushy incidents usually occur beyond the physical proximity of the teacher, a signal system does not work. This is the reason a penalty must be imposed.

Penalties

1)   In a physical conflict situation I often ask the bully and the bullied to write down or tape record (for the remedial student) the chain of events leading to the conflict. This is then discussed with both participants present. Ask each person, "What could you have done that might have been a better choice? How will you deal with this situation if it happens again?" If the student does not seem impressed by your discussion, or indicates by his attitude that he will repeat this behavior, then you should perhaps impose an additional penalty.

2)   Have the bully go to the junior high school or to a grade level higher. This puts him in the underdog identity. Tell him to interview five students concerning their feelings about younger students. Work with him to devise three to five questions such as:

> 1) How do you think 5th graders are different from 8th graders?
>
> 2) Would you beat up a fifth grader if he made you mad? Why or why not?
>
> 3) How do you usually persuade someone smaller than you to do what you want them to?

As he listens to these older students, perhaps he will understand how his behavior has intimidated his peers and other students younger than himself. He may find himself identifying with the underdog students when he hears older students expressing their opinions about kids his own age. This penalty will have to be pre-arranged with the junior high school counselor or the upper level classroom teacher. The bully should report his conclusions back to the class, perhaps at extrapolations.

3)   The bully could look up the rules of boxing or wrestling. He could then report to the class about this sport, emphasizing the difference between it and street fighting.

4)   The bully can help the P.E. specialist with a younger class. Arrangements must be made with the specialist for this idea. Associating with younger kids in a positive way may set up new patterns of socialization for the bully.

5)   Involve the bully in a small discussion group which meets weekly with the school guidance counselor.

6)   Restrict an extra privilege such as eating with friends at noon or playing with certain people during supervised free time. Assign classroom tasks (such as arranging bookshelves, cleaning cupboards) for recess time if there seem to be too many confrontations during recess.

7)   Beat your head against the blackboard. If all else fails, consult the principal for aid. A principal in one of my schools had a signed agreement with bully and parents which specified that the next time the bully physically attacked another child, he would be spanked by the principal. For this particular child, the treatment was effective. The physical punishment seemed to be the only kind to which the bully could relate. This procedure is a big no-no now days with the current rulings on school physical punishment. Fortunately, if the average bully is handled consistently, other "means" will triumph.

The Tattletale

Most teachers don't need extensive bugging systems. If they are the least bit lucky, each year, with no extra charge or PTA dues, awaiting them on the freshly typed white roll sheets will be a name that is synonymous with "Tattletale". On the first day of school you recognize the student immediately by her earphones. And there are other traits: the eraser on her pencil has a microphone (her erasophone), she scored in the sonar range on the hearing test, her purse is shaped like a tongue, she vacations in Cuba, and she takes notes during tether ball. The only misfortune to befall the proud teacher/owner of this alert system is the sporadic playback regulator; this malfunction causes the information to be dispelled at too-frequent intervals and for little or no reason. If she were on warranty, you could return

30

the goods or simply call the repairman. However, the PTA invoice specifies "No refunds, No returns". This clause forecloses the discriminating right of customers to inspect, evaluate, and select all goods before the September 1st inventory. What a bummer!

During approximately the fifth time in one hour that the tattletale appears at your side whispering her devious ear-bolting messages, you will want to cut out her tongue and send it to medical science for erradication of aphasia.

Instead of drawing forth your Swiss army knife with special detonguing attachment, you will calmly approach the problem as a mature but desperate adult.

Possible Solutions

1)   Since you are usually alone with tattletale when she divulges her juicy news, it is easy to talk with her without the knowledge of the other students. (First persuade her to remove her earphones and turn off her erasophone.) Ask her how many times she has been up to see you today? Then ask her how many total interruptions it would make if the whole class tried it? You could point out that not only does it monopolize your teacher time, but it imposes upon the students' time. Ask the student whether the problems she reports are of vital concern to her (often a tattler will report incidents that only effect peers in the classroom, but do not effect the tattler herself.) Impress upon the tattletale that you do not appreciate her telling you things every few minutes. Ask her how she would decide which times to report to the teacher. After she answers, tell her that you only expect her to tell you something about someone once a day, and after that, she should not tell.

2)   If the above does not penetrate (even with the help of sonar) have another conference. Review the reasons why you do not wish her to tattle. You may wish to add that you have noticed other students do not appreciate her tattling, and that you think she would have more friends without doing so. If she is having problems interrelating, tell her that she must work out her own relations, that you would be glad to listen and advise her from time to time, but that you don't enjoy hearing her constantly complain.

A more concrete way to bring about change is to have the student write down on paper (or tape record for those with learning disabilities) vital problems and give them to you at a certain time each day. Do not allow her to tattle. When she attempts to tattle to you, tell her firmly that you are not interested in listening to her but that you would like to read her list after school. Schedule a weekly conference to discuss the lists; in discussing them later, the student often sees the pettiness of her complaints.

Penalties

The worst penalty imposed upon the tattler is not having a receptive confidante. When teachers refuse to participate to any degree, the tattler sooner or latter gives up, or finds another outlet (try any other problem category in this book) for recognition.

THE QUIET ONE

"Are there really Indians in Seattle?" the tall boy with curly hair in New York asked. That's the way they think about Seattle in New York.

The quiet one in your class probably thinks things like that about Seattle all the time, or even worse, but he would never think of actually verbalizing those strange thoughts as did the tall boy with curly hair in New York. The too quiet student may need to be encouraged to express himself more frequently, be it about Seattle, Indians, detente, or where popcorn comes from.

The world is full of all kinds of people from sound barrier breakers and decibel devastators to the common verbal vaccum, and the quiet one is an important part of the sound composite. One may ask why the school feels the need to program each student to be orally outgoing? Due to established norms of sound wave in the typical classroom, the teacher must plunge on to assimilate the too quiet one into this noise-polluted society by encouraging him to also pipe up.

With due concern, there are those students who need to strengthen their self-concepts in the oral language arts area. It is a matter of balancing decibels and confidence. There are many ways a teacher can encourage and reinforce these people. Verbal handicaps such as stuttering, lisping, or other speech impediments are oftentimes at the root of the problem for the quiet one. A student with cleft palate may tend to be the quiet one. Speech therapists will work with these students, but there are beneficial activities which you may also provide in the classroom.

Possible Solutions

1) Put the quiet ones in positions of authority (for instance on small committees, buzz groups, or in charge of collecting for various funds.)

2) The quiet ones seldom volunteer for role playing, so sometimes you may want to have all the class role playing simultaneously in small groups, then choose the quiet one's group to reenact their situation before the entire class.

3) Ask the quiet one to narrate various tapes that you prepare for classes, or give spelling words to small groups of students.

4)   Have the quiet one do some lower grade one-to-one tutoring or tell stories weekly to the primary grades. Arrange this with the librarian or another teacher.

5)   In affective discussions, delegate certain times when you ask every student in the class to give his opinion on an issue. When all students are speaking up, the quiet one is often less inhibited, and will surprise all of you.

6)   For the child with specific verbal disabilities such as the speech impediments mentioned previously, it is necessary to provide extra encouragement. When a child such as this has spoken before the class, make sure that you offer the same constructive criticism that you would offer to all students. Correct improper speech patterns gently from time to time in order that the child continues to develop good habits of speech. Find out what the therapist is working on and attempt to reinforce it daily. At the same time as you correct him, however, compliment him for his improvement and other strengths. Discourage other class members from taunting or mimicing the child with speech problems.

THE SLOW STUDENT

Smart Cookies and Short Cakes

Not all of us were academic child prodigies in our youth. In fact, many of us suffered under the degradation of a "dumb kid" label. Nowdays, though, we refer to that category as "the slower members of the class". We all know that these kids are slow, remedial, or academically behind for thousands of different reasons: perhaps lack of interest, low intelligence, poor nutrition, lack of confidence, poor concentration or listening habits, slow physical or social maturation, family or personal problems to name a few. But no matter why these kids are slow or behind, there is a problem in helping them to progress or catch up academically. It is a problem because in order to help them, much individual teaching is required. Special materials and lessons are necessary, yet at the same time, the students must not become too alienated from their peers. There is much excellent literature published for dealing with slow students, and it is possible to receive special training in working with them. However, most regular classroom teachers receive little help in dealing with their slow students, and the problem is highly discouraging as they view students entering and leaving their classrooms one year later at the same level of incompetence.

Elementary educators tend to consider the slow or remedial classification student as restricted to academics. Most teachers realize that education of the physical body is important too, and it is a part of the curriculum. Sometimes we have the problem of working with a normally-adjusted academic student who is slow in the area of motor skills. The problem in this category is the kid who lost out when coordination quotas were distributed; he has trouble walking around and he acts as though he couldn't care less about improving the situation. P.E. to him is a major event to be avoided. This low potential area causes much frustration, especially if a student is accustomed to high achievement in other areas. For more specific ideas in this area, refer to the chapter on The Physically Disabled Student, page 56

For ease of identification and clarity, I will designate two subjective categories of slow students: (1) The slow student with definite intellectual potential, (2) The slow student who lacks intellectual potential. The manner in which you work with slow students reflects your judgement of their apptitude. It is reasonable to approach all slow students with challenging situations, but it will be highly discouraging to both you and the student if unreasonable expectations are envisioned. The art of working with these students is in encouraging without discouraging, challenging without hounding. Some students truly baffle you because of their verbal aptness coupled with their severe problems in decoding and encoding. Others may excell in math but fail completely in reading. It's hard to know which category they fill; are they potentially normal or are they too burdened with learning disabilities? Are their disabilities associated with only certain areas of learning? I prefer to assume that a slow student has potential if I'm in doubt.

Even if you are relatively certain of a student's potential output, there can exist sub-complications. A slow student with intellectual potential may be unmotivated, requiring a totally different tutelage than his counterpart who is interested in learning. Moreover, the slow student lacking in intellectual potential who is turned-on necessitates different teaching methods than his counterpart who could care less. For this reason, a specific subdivision to "Students With and Without Intellectual Potential" is: (a) the slow student who is interested in learning, and (b) the slow student who is not interested in learning.

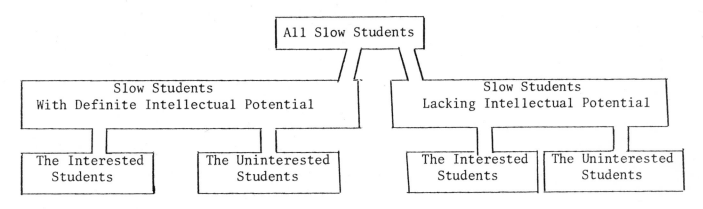

Now this may seem totally hit and miss, unscientific and confusing. It is.

But so is all teaching. If charts such as this were not devised, it could be even less organized. For the unspecialized classroom teacher, not an expert in LD problems or psychological idioscyncrasies, this method seems the clearest most positive way to tackle a discouraging but common classroom problem. In the field of special education, there exist many terms for the slow student. The "slow learner" is often defined as a student with subaverage abilities, and a child who does poorly in school but has normal ability can be referred to as an "underachiever". However, there is controversy about these labels. To most classroom teachers, a slow student is a slow student is a slow student, regardless of the official label. It all boils down to subjectively identifying and dealing with these slow students, no matter what their academic nomeclature. The alternative to using such subjective methods is to ignore the whole messy situation, move the kid on, and keep the cogs clean. We've seen a lot of that in the past few eras of education, and the results are petrifying. This chart merely helps the teacher sort out possibilities and teaching styles for a few displaced, suffering students. It says nothing for the rest of the "normal" class members.

Possible Solutions for Dealing With:

The Slow Student With Definite Intellectual Potential
The Interested Variety

In areas where the slow but promising student shows interest, substantial gains may occur. Some may wonder why an interested student would be slow in the first place? It could be that this student has only recently turned-on to school (perhaps through your inspiration) and has much catching up to do. Or it could be that this student is slow but uninterested in all disciplines except one; if he shows interest only in math, for example, then you will encourage him more specifically in this area. The difficulty is in finding the time to provide positive experiences for the student: time to plan specific lessons, to execute them, and for following up on them. Here are some ideas that will possibly enable you to offer encouraging experiences for your slow yet enthused students with the minimum of superhuman effort.

1)   The first remedy is to encourage and praise the efforts of the slow student around-the-clock. Since this variety of slow student has potential, it is kosher to gently push him on to greater heights while praising recent work.

2)   Notify parents about positive progress via Friday Notes (see page 75 in the chapter covering Zero Self-Concept). Share work with the class, and make sure lots of people know how well the student is progressing. Make sure that the student knows that lots of people know, too.

3)   Utilize lay help: interested parents, community members, junior high or high school students. You may personally contact parents with whom you have associated, or you may send home invitations with the students to all parents, allowing them to specify areas where they are interested in helping. Some parents like to come into the classroom, while others prefer to do work at home. Many are insecure about working on a one-to-one level with students and need much reassurance. (For more ideas here, see Parent Aids, page 22). Contact secondary school students via counselors or staff acquaintances. Many of these people will gladly give you one to three hours weekly if they are made to feel useful, important, and proficient. Most of them need steady assurance and guidance at the beginning but once they become involved with and committed to the slow student, they will usually define their own perameters, relying upon you for materials and advice rather than the complete structure.

One example of parent use: A mother came in one day a week during a time when the class did creative writing. I showed her how to correct with the kids. She would correct (The kid reads what he wrote orally while the mother looks on. She stops the kid when she sees an error or senses a need for direction. This is discussed, corrected by the kid, and the correction process then continues.). I would give her the names of several kids to see, and if she had more time, she would let any kids who cared to come for corrections. She became involved with several class members, and could relate their progress to me. This was a marvelous help in enabling

ALL SNAILS ARE SLOW   SOME STUDENTS ARE SLOW

the slow students to receive extra help once weekly. It is wise to have lay help work with kids on all levels rather than just slow students, otherwise some students may feel picked upon or penalized if they are constantly chosen to receive extra help. Parental help can be used as a treat or an enrichment for firm-standing students.

4)   Have the slow student tutor first, second, or third graders who are experiencing difficulty in similar or different areas.

5)   Ask the slow student to do a surprise talk or presentation in his special field of interest. Perhaps it's motorcycles, horses, diving, or oragami. Use him as an esteemed resource person. Invite the principal or a subject-related specialist (like the P.E. specialist or the art specialist) to hear the presentation. The student could also do his thing for another classroom or even the PTA.

6)   The remedial or slow student with potential is a joy to work with when he is enthused or really trying hard. The most successful trick in helping him is maintaining that enthusiasm and providing chances for success the whole school year long. This continuous effort is exhausting and near impossible, and that was probably the genesis of this student's problems way back when....

Possible Solutions for Dealing With:

The Slow Student With Definite Intellectual Potential
The Uninterested Variety

The day that the principal finds you in the coat closet at 4:00 p.m. wearing crossing guard safety hats, eating dingdongs, yo-yos and odiferously mellowing tuna sandwiches as you sing the second stanza of "Oh, Johnny Oh!" is probably the exact same day that you attempted to work with "the slow student who has potential but is uninterested. This endeavor could be mildly termed as "useless". However, have you a surplus of uselessly designated time, feel free to try some of these ideas in hopes of converting him to the "interested" sect:

1) Use any suggestions in the interested section prior to this, except perhaps lay aid (see solution number 4 for an explanation of this). These ideas probably won't work on this variety of student, but maybe you'll fool both yourself and the student in pretending that you feel he is interested.

2) Have a chat with the disinterested student. Sometimes this student will welcome a chance to discuss his frustrations. Sometimes it just burns him out more. If you can inspire the student, fire him up, or win his vote, then you will be able to try some techniques in the interested section.

3) Call the parents in for a conference. Find out what you can. If you think it important, include the student. However, hashing over the student's remedial standing and his disinterested behavior in his presence probably won't bring about a zesty change. In the parent conference, it is good to discover the student's background, and to check parent response. Some parents tend to view the problem as a thing the student will outgrow, and prefer to have the teacher maintain a liassez-faire policy. Others become very upset or defensive; calm these people and try to agree to a method that will encourage the student to be more interested in school. Some parents are perfect: understanding and supportive. They know that there are multitudes of uncalculable causes to their child's apathy and learning difficulties. In summary, it is best to come to a consensus about the child's problem with the

parents. If they would like more direct action on your part, then they must be made to understand that no progress is possible unless their child will cooperate also. Brainstorming ideas with them to get the child motivated might be helpful; choosing one particular area of reinforcement can be successful when emphasized both at home and school---a way to get the student more excited about himself. Should the conference reveal apathetic parents or parents who feel the responsibility is totally yours and not their little darling's, then it is correct to smile, carry on, and hope for a miracle. Few people will break through the hardened, failure-tested barriers to learning which have been erected by the slow, uninterested student, especially when the home environment offers no support.

4)   Outside help? Profitable use of parents or specialists with the disinterested student is often discouraging. When the student is openly unreceptive to his helpers, he is wasting his and their time. It doesn't hurt to attempt utilizing extra help, but it may be best to hold off until the student indicates he is willing to cooperate with his tutors. Meanwhile, set lots of secret, tantalizing snags for your uninterested students in hopes of enticing them into the sticky gingerbread

house of compulsive studentdom. Just when you least expect it, they'll be nibbling at the frosted eves and you'll be able to help them lick the beaters.

Possible Solutions for Dealing With:

The Slow Student Lacking Potential
The Interested Variety

The public schools have devised many exciting methods for identifying and dehumanizing your typical low potential students. The most extreme cases will usually be referred to special education classes, or spend some time in learning disability classes. You would think that all classrooms would be apple pie normal. But then you always have those borderline cases which fit nowhere, or the transient families who move in and out every three or four months with their nine subfunctional kids. These kids add lots of spark to the classroom, but many times they are not able to operate even minimally no matter how hard they try. It is not only difficult for you as the teacher to provide special lessons for them, but heartbreaking to see the social trauma they experience as they increasingly sense their inabilities in comparison to their "normal" peers. The ability to learn for these kids is severly limited.

So how can you deal with these generally defined low potential students who indicate an interest in school and try again and again and again? And again?

1)   Ironically, all of the suggestions applying to the high potential interested student also apply to the low potential interested student. The main difference will be the degree to which you encourage quality output. It all becomes relative according to your appraisal of the student's utmost abilities. Another factor will be the amount of independence expected of the student; the slow low potential student functions better when someone helps him outline a solid structure. Consider both of these points when applying high potential techniques to the low potential student.

2)   When a kid is already trying his guts out and can't pull the load, something has to be done. The idea is to keep him enthused, encouraged, and to set realistic yet challenging goals for him. This may seem mundane, but it is essential if the kid is way behind. The setting of realistic goals may mean completely changing

regular class assignments everyday or going over every stitch of work as it is assigned to ensure proper understanding. Impossible.

3) If possible, place the child in appropriate achievement level areas for core curricular areas. You may choose to do some team teaching and placement with other teachers; it works great for low math and reading students.

4) If the child is stuck with you and your self-contained classroom, then it means more time on your part because you must design individual assignments for the student. If this is not done, the student will be unable to satisfactorily do the written work, and will be constantly behind.

On one occasion a mentally retarded child was placed in my "regular" classroom. It was horrifying to see his lack of potential, but glorifying to work with him because he never gave up. The other kids grew to adore him, and never batted an eye if they noticed me cutting the child's ten question assignment down to one or two questions. They knew why. Probably the reason the kids were so empathetic was due to our open discussions each morning, and to the emphasis in our classroom on the best qualities of their peers. Criticism was evident, but it was directed in the positive vein. It took much work to help this low child, and both he and I were often frustrated in meeting his needs. Whether my inadequate training in teaching the disabled was detrimental to this child or whether his positive development in a normal environment was overriding is a long-standing question.

5) Once again, emphasize the positive. Let the student know when you are pleased.

6) If you can't seem to teach a skill on the one-to-one basis (such as borrowing or telling time), ask a student to try it. Tell the student that you are feeling discouraged about the way you've been teaching "Harry" and ask if he can help you. Tell him what it is that you want taught. This technique also works well in different situations. For example, you may have just explained a new concept in math or science. Ask how many kids think they are a little tiny bit confused. Send a child who understands the concept to work with each student who is confused. It's noisy,

but within minutes the number of comprehenders is doubled. Repeat the process until everyone gets it. Within five minutes at least ten more "I've got it!" lights will be flashing. Aren't kids bananas?

7)   Ask the child to go over a few papers for you. Choose something very structured for him to evaluate, such as the coloring of maps, neatness, or simple math problems. Or ask him to make a ditto for you about a certain subject. Use it in a presentation. This makes the child feel great, and it makes you feel great too.

8)   If the kid is a for real slowy, you owe it to him, his parents, and yourself to refer him. Go through the proper channels, levels, and school hassles. If your set up is good, perhaps there is an LD classroom or special education situation that will prepare him more suitably for his future. You cannot be expected to completely meet this child's needs in the regular classroom; too much individual time is necessary.

9)   Another important point: In order to prevent the midyear fury of the "But you never told us!" syndrome from frustrated parents, it is infinitely wise to invite the parents in for a conference during the first two months of school to let them know their child is seriously behind his peers. If you wait until the first fall report, it often comes as a shock or a threat, and the parents will be upset that they were not notified before. Many parents will hire tutors or take great prophylactic steps in anticipation of a rough year if they are but informed early. If you are teaching in the intermediate level, most parents will already be aware of their child's difficulties, and have been frozen in suspense awaiting your call. They usually come to the conference with an organized list of reasons why their little dear is behind, and you know that you will be a future contributing cause to his demise when they go to their next year's teacher with the same rumpled, sorry excuses. For parents it is too painful to say, "I really don't know why our child is experiencing so much difficulty," when a reason makes it all so simple.

Possible Solutions for Dealing With:

The Slow Student Lacking Potential
The Uninterested Variety

This is a space case. The wisest thing is not to waste too much valuable time with this problem. Try the possible solutions as listed under the slow student with definite potential, heading quickly to a parent conference and early referral. It is like a seventy mile uphill bicycle trip, and if you make it to the summit, you will coast down the other side. Rarely, however, do you make it that far without daily training, preparation, and a positive attitude by all participants.

THE THIEF

It's always that "invaluable name-engraved new red pencil with the gold lettering that has never even ever been sharpened with a new pink eraser that I just got yesterday that my dad gave me for cleaning up the pigeons' cage for three weeks while he was away doing business in Argentina..." or the "brand new squeaky clean multi color, effervescent set of UniMart Sale Daze washable all-purpose magic marker pens with duripress hard tip and ever-spring color-coded caps that my big sister gave me for my birthday just last week when I was eleven..." Yes, it's always those items which mysteriously disappear right between math and social studies, or right after noon recess. The whole class loyally joins forces in the giant game of dragnet, but alas, no goods are recovered.

That's one version. There are several exciting variations:

Variation A: Confidential Cathy whispers to you that she saw the thief take that pencil right out of John's desk...

Variation B: You thought Pat was acting strange last period---and he has red and green felt pen all over his clothes (Common knowledge that Pat does not own a set of pens).

Variation C: You have no tangible evidence, but you had suspected Brad in previous incidences, and feel that once again he is the one.

So now, how do you solve the mystery and prevent it from occurring in the

near future?

Possible Solutions

1)   You are best-off if you have proof of the guilt. As soon as a loss is
reported, use clues to solve it by your own hunches. If you suspect someone
strongly (maybe Joe sat at Tom's desk during science), call the suspect to you, and
ask him to please open his desk so that both of you can look inside together. Try
to do this at recess, or at a time when other students are not in the vicinity. If

the child refuses to open his desk, it may bring about the tearful admission that he is hiding someone else's property. Or, it could bring about a fierce denial that there is anything to hide in his desk and that he refuses to open it anyway. Asking the child to open his desk immediately tells him that you suspect him, so if nothing is found, you should tell him how relieved you are, because you did not wish to suspect him of such dishonesty. If he refuses to cooperate then you must tell him that you feel he is hiding something and will always wonder about his integrity. Tell him he is free to talk with you about this problem at any time. Then let it go. However, if the item is found, you should ask him if he knows whose property the pencil is, and how did it get into his desk? Then, you should tell him that you are sorry this happened, that it is very serious to take other people's belongings. Tell him that if this happens again, he will have to face a penalty.

You may suggest or insist that he apologize and confess to the child from whom he stole. This could be left up to you or him---some students will be humilated enough and forever deterred merely from being discovered. Others will better remember the pain of it all if they are forced to face the peer. This experience is not pleasant, but it is effective if positively and honestly executed.

2)   One additional hint: If the thief chooses (or is instructed) to apologize and confess to the child from whom he stole, you might speak with the victim immediately before or after to insure a positive response. Help the victimized child to empathize with the thief. This chat may not be necessary if the victim is unusually sensitive to the situation.

3)   What about the persistent, irreconcilable thief who refuses to be reformed? This child, even when caught red-handed, may deny her thievery or repeat it again at the next opportunity. If you have tried solutions number one and two and still the problem is acute, then perhaps it would be judicious to involve the school counselor. The intense involvement of professional therapy could be your only recourse. In the meantime, watch the thief like a hawk for two reasons: to protect your personal belongings and the belongings of class members, and to prevent opportunities for

further complications in dishonesty.

4)   At times you will be unable to solve the case of the missing pencil. Even though you may suspect a certain student, there is nothing to be done unless you have specific evidence. When frequent occasions arise where items are missing, it is best to open up the problem to the class. At a class meeting, present the situation or ask a class member to introduce it: "Many items have been missing each week in this class. What kind of problem do we have?" (Lack of trust, dishonesty...) Direct discussion towards definition of the problem and possible prevention of its continuation: "How can we prevent this from happening so often?" Discuss as well possible reasons why students think someone would want or need to take their belongings. Use role playing, letting students act out why they as a thief would take an item not belonging to them. This may make the thief understand her problem more fully, and give her an opportunity to relive it incognito. After you feel that the students have an empathy for the thief, discuss what the students suggest that the thief do to receive positive, encouraging help with her social problem: "If you wanted to help the thief get rid of her or his problem, what would you suggest she or he do?" (Talk to the teacher, a class leader, or counselor...) "Do you think the thief should be punished if she or he comes for help?" Discussions such as this may help the thief to realize that the class wants to eradicate the problem and also help her through tempting situations. This discussion could be held in several sessions, or be repeated with various emphases over a time period in order to reinforce its therapeutic benefits.

Penalties

1)   For crimes of small consequence, such as pencils or rubberbands, most kids will be deterred by having to "fess up" or in knowing that the teacher regularly reads "Spy vs Spy". (Why do kids like to steal rubberbands? I once had a rubberband fanatic in my class. Each day she would try to make it out the door with her coat pockets stuffed with wriggling rubberbands. When caught, she would sheepishly

but disappointedly return them to the box in the cupboard. Maybe she sold them on the elementary school black market.)

2)   For prime crime, the victim should be reimbursed. If milk money has been rifled, then it should be repaid. A Gucci purse should not be replaced by a Pucci scarf. If the item is very expensive, such as a radio, then likely the parents must be contacted and involved. Usually the act of reimbursing or earning the money is sufficient punishment. Thieves find it hard to drop their old habits. If you are smart, you will remember this and attempt to afford as few opportunities as possible for further incidents.

BROWN NOSE

Me? Have pets? You must be crazy!

Teachers never recognize their pets to themselves. They may admit that certain students are charming or more fun to work with, but they are positive that they do not overly favor these propitious students.

"Not so," says the class. The class knows who the brown nose is. The brown nose knows how to talk with you on an adult level, and can bend your ear on the stiffest day. This sycophant swoozles you while Priscilla is passing out her birthday treats and no one else will even listen to your pleas. The brown nose will clean the sink after painting and leaves the brushes in the coffee can with the bristles up. Why does the brown nose do this?

You: Because she's just a downright nice kid.

The class: Because she's teacher's pet and she can get away with everything.

So how can you solve a problem that you can hardly admit that you have, and moreover, one that doesn't really bother you personally? One nice thing about elementary school brown noses: they usually are helpful and affectionate truly because they are enamoured to you, not for ulterior motives. Because of this innocent feature, it is even more difficult to "let go" in the closeness of your rapport.

1)   If you even slightly suspect that you are victim of indenture to a brown nose (such as the usual outright and truthful accusation by that tactful loudmouth who says, "Yeah...you <u>always</u> have Sue do that for you because she's your pet." Shocked look, silent opening and closing of mouth in agitation), then it's probably true. So, you must change. Do not always ask Sue to do it. Ask someone else. Pretend that Sue is absent for a week or two. Do <u>anything</u>, but for sure don't do it with Sue.

2)   Try having the class select runners and other such monitors. Or try a rotation system. Granted, it's hardly worthwhile having Maury Moron screw up the lunch count for one whole month; certain students seem to have apptitude for certain jobs.

Sometimes, though, a student will surprise you. Sue doesn't always need to help you out, even though it is easier because she catches on fast, is neat, organized, and likes that sort of thing.

3)   Some students definitely do not get off on helping the teacher, running errands, or doing clerical favors. Don't force them. There should be plenty of other kids who would like to staple. Remember that Sue is absent.

4)   Suspect that you truly do have a brown nose in your midst, in the eyes of the class at least, and try not to fulfill their masochistic fantasies by reinforcing their hopeful suspicions.

THE ATTENTION STARVED ONE

Suddenly you feel a 50 pound blow between the shoulder blades. It only brings back the familiar recollection of Jennifer. Jennifer expresses her affection in the most overt manner. It's like a love pat from a grizzly. Then there's spidery, snakey Mary with those spring-loaded pipecleaner arms which attach themselves to your trunk or arms, entwine, and squeeze you breathless. For comic relief, you are fortunate to have with you Kent's "Three Stooges Act", which he runs every two minutes or so, complete with hand gestures and chapped-lips sound track. You were about to say, "That's enough", but then remembered Bart Broadcaster with his top of the news national, state, local, and neighborhood playground parables, familial intimacies, and the room 601 special. He would be great if you could afford a couch alongside your desk and were paid eight hours daily to listen intently. Worst of all, you really do enjoy his commentaries, and find him verbally gifted; it's a pity you don't have more time and energy to devote to his broadcasts.

What do all those people have in common? They are all attention-starved or relatively love deprived. They need someone so badly to listen to them, to hug, or to talk with them that they cannot control their obsessive behaviors. What can you do that will not only enable them to frequently express themselves without becoming overly dependent upon teacher response or demanding too large a portion of the teacher's time, as well as give them a stronger sense of being loved or appreciated?

Possible Solutions for Dealing With:

The Talker

1)   When a loquacious student confides to you in long-play 33 RPM at the beginning of class each day, it becomes irksome. It's best to try listening as much as you can; obviously the student needs an outlet. If the propensity becomes overbearing and you feel the student can handle some on-the-level feelings, tell her why you are unable to talk with her so often and so long. Some students respond well to this. Others may need several straight forward reminders. During the withdrawal stage it helps to have a lunch date scheduled, enabling the student to relate important feelings. Otherwise, a student may feel hurt or neglected, and her problems may be transferred to new areas. You gave your reason for curtailing the monologue monopoly once to the student, but don't be surprised if you find it necessary to repeat your reasons on several occasions. For more ideas about talkers or discussion monopolizers, see page 26 regarding The Bully.

The Show Off

2)   This student isn't necessarily starved for your attention, but for any attention. Usually he will have a repertoire such as frog hops, "Three Stooges," or burps. When his behavior gets to the point of being nauseating and too frequent, you must talk with the student. A class meeting is a good way to solve the problem without getting too specific. The subject of "showing off" is a familiar one to kids, and they will hash it out, maybe even mentioning the problem in their midst. If this is not the remedy preferred by you to negate the pattern, a private conference would be best. Sometimes I have even told kids that they can to their "thing" once daily, but that's all. If your talk has been strict enough, that should settle it.

If penalties must be imposed, you may restrict privileges. Isolating the show off before the rest of the class or reprimanding him openly only reinforces his actions. Therefore it is best to remain very cool in your dealings.

Here is one effective idea for controlling a show off, especially one who verbally interrupts during large group discussions. After the show off has imposed his interruptions two or three times upon the group, quietly whisper to him that you would like him to help you with a secret poll which will be announced to the class later. Tell him to keep tally during the rest of the lesson on how many times someone interrupts someone else or speaks out, or interferes without being courteous to others. No matter if the other students are curious about this; it gives Show Off some positive recognition, a purpose, and helps him to realize the distracting effects of someone who constantly interrupts. Let Show Off present his tabulations at the close of the lesson; it will give him a chance for the lime light and also allow him the opportunity to explain the conclusion of his tallies, restating your

desires for a more ordered environment.

The Physical Leech

3)   These persons usually hug, fondle, or squish you. Often they like to climb onto your lap or latch on to your arms or hands as you walk. In my classroom some students used to style my hair while I read stories to the class after lunch. Sometimes I found myself braided to a chair or was disturbed by painful tugs as I read. Selected amounts of physical affection between student and teacher is good, but sometimes a student may become too dependent on it. If you feel the need to discourage an over-affectionate student, you may quickly walk away from him after a warm grasp, pat, or hug. Whenever you pass the affection-deprived student's desk, put your hands on his shoulders or give him a quick hug with your eyes. This will offer frequent physical contact and let the student know that you still like him, even if you do brush him off rather tartly during his clingier moments. At times when you are caught in a stationery position, such as in a sprawling group on the floor, it is necessary to tell everyone to "back off" to prevent stuffiness or pile ups. A big overstuffed Goodwill chair will allow five or six cuddlers to drape themselves around you comfortably.

The Tackler

4)   When your neck is stiff for two days following the latest burst of affection, it's time to tranquilize your admirer. Tacklers are so robust in their sincerity that it takes your breath away. With overt kids such as this, it's usually quite easy to be direct. Simply tell them that you appreciate their enthusiastic greetings, but that it is an unpleasant shock to be patted so forcefully. Explain that they are underestimating their strength, that you do not enjoy the sensation and that you would appreciate it if they would be more gentle.

THE PHYSICALLY DISABLED

Joanne was in fifth grade, was 5'8" tall, and weighed 135 pounds. She was long-limbed and womanly. Having Joanne in class was fun because she was exactly my height; we compared fashions, traded shoes for the day, and talked about the infinite advantages of being tall. When Joanne needed to get a drink from the knee-high water fountain in our room, she was forced to perform veritable calesthentics to reach the awkward level of the pathetic dribble of water without allowing the whole class to see far up her skirt. When Joanne sat writing away at her desk, her knees calmly draped onto the floor at the place where most kids' tootsies were dangling. But Joanne always carried herself straight and tall, and loved to look me in the eye with her cheerful glimmer. Joanne's physical reality somewhat disabled her at the water hole, but no one could hope to challenge her in touch football.

For most kids, physical disabilities are a serious matter. Even for Joanne it was important to constantly work at building her esteem so that she wouldn't feel too Amazonish amidst her 4'4" peers. Effectively utilizing the disabled student's skills during physically prohibitive or limited activities is sometimes trying, but with some forethought is usually feasible. The most important idea is to find something for the student to do that requires responsibility, the feeling of being needed, and the opportunity for skill growth and development.

Possible categories under "physically disabled" within the elementary classroom might be: 1) real illness, 2) pseudo or psychosomatic illness, 3) temporary or permanent loss of limbs, 4) limited vision or hearing, 5) motor retardation or cerebral palsy, 6) chronic diseases such as diabetes, asthma, and allergies, 7) hyperactivity, 8) erratic developmental growth, 9) congenital deformity.

Illness may cause students to become academically and physically behind, to lack social confidence, or to dwell unnecessarily upon their condition. Some students tend to be slightly neurotic when it comes to their health, imagining or creating a fine variety of illnesses. Others, such as those with asthma, have been so overly-protected that they fear normal physical activity. Still others may ignore their sickness or resulting weakness and over-exert. After an illness, it is important to be aware of all these facets and to instill within students a healthy outlook about their bodies.

Possible Solutions for Dealing With:

Real Illness

1)   How do you know when to send a sick child home? Most schools relieve you of this responsibility, assigning the task to the nurse or secretary. This is logical, since time must be taken to assess the symptoms, contact parents, and arrange transportation. Meanwhile, you are teaching this and that and don't really have enough time to concern yourself with all of the details concerning the sick child. The best a teacher can do is to offer a sympathetic ear and an observant eye to the child's malaise, send a class buddy with her to the office, and make sure she receives prompt, appropriate help.

Highly contagious diseases such as impetigo or ringworm should be collared as soon as possible. When you see an open sore or suspicious rash for several consecutive days, it is wise to refer the child to the school nurse. If the nurse is in the building only once a week, this is difficult. In those instances, a courteous, concerned call to the parent requesting medical follow-up is appropriate.

Whether a child has been out of school for an extensive period and missed the majority of work or merely absent two days, he must be reassimilated as soon as possible so that he will not feel disoriented. Requiring him to make-up each assignment is stringent, usually unprofitable because he will feel too discouraged, which leads to sloppy output. In subjects such as math, it is necessary to complete a certain amount of practice work but for other subjects, establishment of the main concept should be sufficient. A quick but thorough way to catch a child up on the main concept ideas is to ask another enthusiastic, verbal student to tell the returning student all about what has been happening within a certain subject area. Let him use old assignments, filmstrips, or teaching aids. This half hour or so with child-to-child explanation will often fill in the missing links.

Not only is there a certain amount of lesson work to be caught up on, but there is the whole process of social and psychological adjustment to the return. Reaffiliation to class activities is the most crucial aspect, for all other output rests upon the healthy attitude of the student. Helping him to adjust confidently to changes that may have occurred in his absence is the best remedy. This can be done by talking privately with him before class, summarizing various and possibly upsetting things that happened (for example, "We decided to move all the desks to the other side of the room," or "You're now in a different math group until we are sure you are caught up...") so that the student can react to you in instances that may be threatening. A good buddy may also fill in here, but when the news tends to orient him about John's latest batch of firecrackers or Sue's uncle's rat poison instead of telling him what has actually taken place in his absence, it isn't too helpful. In most cases the student likes to walk into class after his two month absence and have everyone act as though he had been gone a few minutes on an errand. Your debriefing can enable him to do this more sauvely. It's totally necessary to be cool and casual.

Another problem with real illness may occur when the super athlete returns from a serious convalescence. This student may overcompensate by participating too enthusiastically in a game or sport in order to be macho athlete. At this time it is good to think of an excuse to remove the student from the game a few minutes, allowing rest, without making him feel like a weakling in front of his friends. You could send him back to the classroom for a whistle, ask him to referee for you for awhile, or have him observe for a certain skill to be demonstrated by an exemplary peer. A verbal reminder to "take it easy" is oftentimes ignored or begrudged.

In cases where a child has been absent over a week's time, sending limited assignments home via parents of siblings will enable him to keep abreast in a few academic areas. Discussions or pertinent class activities could be taped to provide the student with a feel for things that have taken place in his absence. The

quantity of work sent home should be gauged according to the student's level of convalescence; parents will often be able to estimate how little or much work should
be sent home. If a student is absent for lengthy periods of time at frequent intervals, such as a victim of leukemia, then he will probably be unable to wholly catch-
up at any point. Many school districts will install bedroom-to-classroom radios,
enabling the student to follow as much as he is able of the daily classroom events.
When a child is bedridden for weeks at a time, it is uplifting for the teacher to
visit the child at home, remembering to tuck in a little something special to hasten
the speedy recovery. Letters from the kids at school are a treat for the ill child;
he can enjoy these as he also learns the latest gossip.

Pseudo Illness

2) Pseudo illness is fascinating and dangerous ground from the teacher's point
of view. Some students prefabricate illnesses or exaggerate their difficulties in
order to gain attention or to avoid doing certain tasks or activities. This psychosomatic tendency should be quickly perceived and remedied before it victimizes both
student and teacher.

The judgement of "when it's time to do something about it" is purely subjective on the part of the teacher. This is difficult to carry out because of possible neurotic parent support. One example occurred when a student brought parental
notes frequently which excused her from gym, such excuses as sinuses, twisted
ankles, or a new dress. The climax to these happenings unfolded one day when she
brought a note excusing her from P.E. because of an "injury to her foot". After
watching her chase six boys in seven directions at recess, I was suspicious. So I
discreetly asked to see said injury. This "condition" in actuality was a drying,
nearly healed blister covered by a bandaid. Hence I told the child that I had indeed read her mother's note, but that I did not feel the condition warranted skip-
ping P.E. because she could go without her shoes in the gym if she liked. I also
pointed out that her parents had been informed by school publications that the only

valid excuse from P.E. class would be a doctor's note. Therefore I would make the decision. Actions such as this can cause a fair amount of fervor by angry parents, so I always make it a point to notify parents during orientation that their child will not be excused from P.E. without a doctor's note, and that in case of a parent note, I will feel obligated to judge whether the child should participate or not.

Another case brought to mind is the child who refused to sit on the floor or rug because of her allergies. This was touchy, but with this particular child I felt there were tendencies to exaggerate conditions in order to get attention. Therefore, I insisted she join us on the rug. It could have been disastrous. However, I had a sound knowledge of notes in the child's health record, and had held several conferences with the mother concerning the child's various (and numerous, according to mom) disabilities. Sometimes you can take those chances and you win. Other times you lose. Before taking the chance, it is best to be factually informed. The danger of not taking a chance is in allowing the child to think that she can control and manipulate situations by certain conditions of her health. Children learn quickly which people they can dupe. They will usually not try their sick routine once they realize you are on to them. When in doubt about how to deal with a seemingly psychosomatic problem, rather than taking a risk, a teacher had best seek the aid of a qualified professional, be it a physician, counselor, or nurse.

Many times a child will come to you complaining of a headache or stomach upset, asking that he be allowed to go to the nurse. It is impossible to deny this privilege to a child, for he may truly feel ill. However, if this seems to happen too frequently at regular times (such as during spelling tests), a special arrangement should be made with the nurse or secretary. Such physical manifestations may truly be experienced by the child due to nervous anxiety, but somehow a pattern should be established to break the habit. Perhaps the child should either be sent home (which he may not like) or obligated to participate in class activities.

With mature intermediate gradeschool females comes the onset of puberty and menstruation. As a result of poor education, this monthly event can be interpreted as an illness by some girls. When a girl seems to be using her period as an excuse to refrain from certain activities, it is time for a person-to-person chat. This is best done female-to-female, so a male teacher may be forced to call upon a counselor, nurse, or secretary for this occasion. The onset of puberty is an exciting, important event to a girl, and can be approached enthusiastically from that standpoint. If the girl is made to feel important and womanly through transmission of this excitement, she will not experience the need to attract attention by feigning weak or ill at the time of her menstruation. A supportive mother may notify you that her daughter is beginning to menstruate or that she expects the onset soon so that you can be especially aware of the possible inconveniences or perplexities

that she may experience. Usually this knowledge is not actively needed, but it is
good to know such information for times that are extraordinary.

Temporary or Permanent Loss of Limbs

3)   For the child temporarily or permanently disabled, perhaps confined to a
cast or wheelchair, have her keep score, time, or referee. If a lengthy recupera-
tion is involved, ask her to design a quiet game for the class (one where she could
participate) or to report on the history of the sport which the rest of the class is
learning. Activities other than P.E. should not be exclusive of the child; accom-
modations can be made. Most kids in casts adapt themselves extraordinarily to their
impediment. They are regarded as folk heroes and enjoy rising to the occasion.
Most often they will choose to try a sport even though they can't do everything.

Limited Vision or Hearing

4)   Limited sight or hearing is crucial to the student in the classroom. Most
difficult from the teacher's standpoint is the mere discovery of the handicap; often
the fact becomes evident by a note from the protective parent, an accidental shuff-
ling through health cards, or the thoroughness of a previous teacher's year-end note.

It is best to privately discuss the loss with the student. She should
know that you are aware of the problem, otherwise she may be too shy to tell you
when she has difficulties. Impress upon her the importance of notifying you when she
is unable to see or hear adequately. Once the problem has been openly discussed between the two of you, it should be easier for the student to deal with the inconvenience naturally.

Motor Retardation of Cerebral Palsy

5)   Most children with cerebral palsy or severe lack of motor development are
sifted out and hidden away from view into special programs. However, there are
cases where a child has been allowed to remain in the regular program for various
reasons. When teaching among the so-called "normal" students, getting your shoes

stepped on or seeing kids fall over every ten minutes or so is nothing new. However, even the "chief normal shoe tromper" will tend to burst into giggles the first time when watching the motor-impaired student run or be physically active. It looks awkward and is sometimes embarrassing or disquieting to the "normal" child to see a physically handicapped person actively participating in sports. The laughing is a cover for the student's social discomfort. Due to this great system's method of hiding away handicapped youngsters, the "normal" child does not often receive the learning chance to observe and understand the disabilities of the handicapped. But no matter how it looks or what the social system, no laughing must be permitted. Kids know that the disabled student is physically handicapped, and should not be allowed to tease her. Instead, they must be encouraged to help her, or to cheer her on when she succeeds. Examples of how to discourage teasing and encourage positive feedback will follow.

A thrilling scene once occurred in my classroom during a fifth grade P.E. class. The class was learning to play volleyball and had practiced serving and volleying for several days. One child, mildly retarded physically and mentally, had experienced momentous difficulties in learning these skills and was obviously a detriment to his team. Upon his turn to serve, he miraculously was able to get it all together, and served successfully. His entire team immediately enfolded him with hugs and cheers, and the grin on his face shot around the world and back. This was the outcome of much systematic coaching with the kids to praise one another when successful, and particularly, the total disapproval of negative comments toward any erring student.

A specific problem in elementary school is integrating the physically disabled student into relays. No one, even when they're "good sports", wants to lose every time because of the disabled student. Therefore, choose one or two kids to sit out during the first race. Then let them replace any other students on any teams before the next race begins. This is easy to do because often there are an uneven amount of participants. Within the rotation of team members, teams become less bent upon winning and the disabled child may be relocated to another team. It also allows tired students to rest and gives variation to patterns of competition. Another use of the disabled kid: let her mark the finish point in races, or place the winners.

When playing other games besides relays, the handicapped child will still be a downer to her team. For this reason, it is best to change team members often. As stressed before, continual emphasis of building skills and positive reinforcement are the best aids in encouraging both the motor retarded student and her peers.

Overall, positive, smiling, enticement is constantly needed to encourage the physically disabled child. Competing and comparing themselves to normally developed children, they are bound to sense their inferior abilities, and will become disinclined to participate if not encouraged. Establishing a supportive climate among the class peers is a task which will require much talking and follow-up by you. The likeability of the disabled child will influence the class' attitude too; however, teachers set the tone in organized activities. Be alert to mimicing and teasing.

Sometimes it is important to speak openly with the class about a disabled or retarded child; kids can understand the causes of motor problems, and will deal in a more adult-like manner with a problem which they are allowed to discuss as adults. If you are afraid to hold a discussion, remember that such conversations will still be held among students in whispering gossip groups and that the benefit of an all-class, well-directed and informed discussion could reverberate throughout the year.

Chronic Illness

6) Chronic diseases such as diabetes, asthma, and allergies under proper medical control will pose few problems for a child in the classroom. With all of these conditions the child may face some dietary restrictions, but activities usually need not be restricted. Harboring a few tootsie rolls in your desk drawer

is a good idea if the diabetic has tendencies towards poor control. The asthmatic should be able to judge the amount of physical activity in which he should participate. Thorough knowledge of these children's health records is essential in making decisions about their exposure to possible dangers. Much emotional support should be lent to these kids as their health situations also present possible psychological complications and these emotional problems can influence the state of their disease.

Hyperactivity

7)   A true disability to the performance level of a child is the tendency toward hyperactivity. This label currently being the rage of the '70's, many students may be plastered into the mold unfairly. Because the definition of the problem is so controversial, it is difficult to know what to do about it. Most hyperactive kids will manifest behavioral patterns which fit into diverse problem categories, and you will try solutions according to the particular behavior. Whether or not you dare to recommend medical referral is a matter you should perhaps discuss first with the guidance counselor; many parents explode when given the indication that their child is hyperactive, fearing the child will be given drugs or experimental treatments.

Erratic Developmental Growth

8)   No two kids mature physically at the same rate. Being abnormally short or tall or fat could be only a temporary disability to the child during a tenuous period of his development. It may or may not physically restrict him to a large degree, but it can cause serious psychological or social problems. Kids dislike being physically different from their peers. Helping them to feel important, to establish a positive self-concept, and to realize the impermanence of their situation are your best alternatives. More solutions for the Fat Kid are found on page 99.

Congenital Deformities

9)   Congenital deformities do not necessarily disable a child physically; more

often the disablement is social. Helping the child to feel accepted and functional in the classroom setting is crucial. Activities which emphasize the ability of the child rather than the limitations of the child are desirous.

THE SNEAK

This student is so slippery that a little dab will do you. He is able to out-maneuver you at any point, and is always missing when you want him. Most famous is his disappearing act after school. He never needs to be dismissed; he merely evaporates. His major defense is the fact that your attention is often distracted. Suddenly you remember that you asked him to talk with you for a moment after school, but he's gone. Not only does he unctuously sneak in this way, but he also likes to ignore homework or deadlines for class work. He consistently turns in work late or incomplete and you're lucky to grab it as it slithers through his greasy little hands. (For more solutions to late classwork, see The Lazy One, page 85). If only you could have a chance to speak with him, perhaps you could alleviate further complications. What you need is a solution for tacking him down.

Possible Solutions

1) Your first goal is actually being able to trap the sneak for a meeting. Indicate to the student that it is very important for him to meet you soon at a private time. Ask the student to suggest a time for the meeting. This involvement on his part may hit home. If he shows up, you will know it is important to continue to allow him the opportunity to make decisions, for he demonstrates that he responds more readily to his own direction.

2) If the above remedy has failed (he slipped by again: no show!), ask the student to sit in your chair at your desk prior to dismissing the class. If possible, give him something helpful to do, such as correcting a paper, organizing a drawer, or recording information. After the class has been dismissed, he will handily be at your desk waiting. Another method is to dismiss the class by using quicky math problems, for example the multiplication tables or "what's 5x3+2-4=?" As each child individually responds to the equation you give her, she is free to go. Leave 'ol sneak until last, and then pop him your big equation. Pretty slick trick.

3) If these methods have failed, give the class a quiet assignment, let them

read, or choose a time when you are not actively needed. Quietly call the student to you, then slip into that Early Salvation Army Recovered Easy Chair, a quiet corner, or the hallway. Hold your discussion.

4)   If daily follow-up is needed to curtail further schlepping about, arrange with the student a time when he should meet with you each day to discuss his responsibilities and commitments. I find that immediately after dismissal is a good time to go over obligations for the next day. It is best to have them listed prior to the meeting (the student does this), and you should sign the list after having reviewed them with the student. If communicating with parents is a problem, it can be helpful to require the student to have the list signed at home, then returned to school the next day. Certain students will play you for every possible break. Let this student know that you expect a reliable commitment on his part, and that you will not accept his excuses. It is difficult to be so hard-nosed, but if you are consistent, it will require only one or two confrontations.

Penalties

1)   If some of the above fails once, try again. But before doing so, tell the student the consequences of his irresponsibility. Let him know that he will pay a price the next time, and if possible, tell him exactly what it will be. In the case of the sneak, there are many feasible penalties. Always consider the needs and personality of the individual student, making the penalty as positive as possible. I prefer having the student devise his own penalty by asking him, "What do you think should happen to you if you fail to show up (or complete the assignment) as we had planned?" The first response by a student will usually be flip or hardline punative, such as "...stay after school..." Encourage the student to think more deeply about it by responding, "Do you think that would be a punishment that would help you with your problem? How would it help you? Can you think of another penalty that would be more helpful to you?" If the student is stuck on that one, you could suggest one of such alternatives as:

Writing down what has happened, why, and what the student could have done to prevent its happening,

Interviewing several school staff members about meeting personal responsibilities and the consequences of not doing so (this could be done by tape recorder for the remedial student),

Researching the term "responsibility", oh how boring,

Leading a class discussion on the importance of keeping a promise,

Lengthening the assignment each time it is late,

Working on regular assignments for a period after school,

Completing custodial tasks for the classroom,

Missing the next big, special activity in class, or missing the activity planned for that day.

Perhaps after having been obligated to complete one or two penalty activities, the student will decide it's easier to meet his obligations rather than constantly sneaking out.

THE GIFTED CHILD

Not only do you have to keep ahead of these rascals, you need to catch up with them in the first place. Many teachers do not wish to recognize that a student has more apptitude in a certain area than do they. This fear is unnecessary. Even if a student demonstrates superior profficiency on subject matter knowledge in a particular area, teachers may still be important learning stimulators by their knowledge and utilization of resource channels and their pervasive encouragement.

It's not too bad if your class has one student who is gifted in only one or two areas, but when you have a full class of several kids gifted in one or two areas, that's a real challenge. Describing a gifted student is not easy, and there are many excellent books concerning the subject. But if you don't have time to read the whole bunch of books, take a gamble and assume you might have a gifted kid in your class. I find that there are many kids gifted in at least one area. With gifted children there is often a high degree of independence (many times related only to that area of interest) and usually they may be advanced in other areas as

69

well. The problem of challenging and fortifying the gifted student doesn't beat down your door when compared to the myriad of other exotic problems knocking away; it just leaves you feeling empty inside because you know you are letting down fine talent. How to find the time and energy to relate more succinctly to your gifted students?

Possible Solutions

1) Capitalize on the child's independence or superior skills in one particular area. Give him chances to work on his own in depth. Presenting projects to other classes or small groups within the classroom is highly stimulating.

2) Utilize paraprofessional help (mothers, aids) within the school as well as district specialists. Do not be timid to call down to that big curricular office, speak with the director, and put her to work for you. These people will often design interesting projects or provide additional opportunities for growth. Many times they are not invited into the classroom to work with actual live kids, and will be thrilled to change their pace by escaping for a few hours from the binders of their own curriculum guides, or unheard of yet, even demonstrating some of the ideas they have been telling you to instigate.

3) Have the gifted student devise various teaching aids for you in her field of interest.

  a. For example, an artistic student may enjoy creating accurate, systematic diagrams to be dittoed and distributed to the entire class.

  b. She could invent a game which reinforces a concept in any curricular area. The game could be played and enjoyed by many class members, positively realigning the gifted child's self-regard and self-worth.

  c. Ask the gifted child to introduce and explain a new concept to the class; math is an excellent area for this, or geography. When a gifted child is put into the position of teaching, she will sometimes appreciate the efforts of the teacher in dealing with the masses and be less impatient in her own learning situations.

70

d. Many times a gifted child will enjoy tutoring on a cross grade level basis. Caution must be taken in over-using the gifted child within her own classroom; student jealousies, rivalries, and accusations of favoratism may develop.

e. Some students gifted in the language arts enjoy the responsibility of handing out needed spelling of words to other students during periods where writing is involved. A schedule may be devised whereby the designated student passes out small tagboard cards to any student needing a word. The students quietly go over to the desk of the person designated to distributed words, asking that student to write the word in question on the card. They may pick up words anytime they need them. Words that have been collected by each student during the year can be used in many ways to individualize the curriculum.

SAMPLE WORD CARD: Approximately 5" x 1-1/2"
                        -Tagboard-

Punch hold for collecting in looseleaf binder---

4) Certain teachers may wish to combine efforts certain times monthly to offer an activity in a specific area for gifted children from several classrooms. This offers gifted students wider experiences. Each teacher may select a few gifted students to participate, and if the arrangement were for one teacher per month to offer an activity in a designated area, the burden would be light for instructors, but rewarding for the gifted child.

5) While most experts in the field of gifted child education disagree, some teachers believe that if children are really gifted, they will fulfill themselves on their own. Teachers have a lot to do, and perhaps their time would be better spent working with the majority or with the remedial children. It all depends upon the propensity of the problem in your eyes: how much time and energy should you delegate

to the needs of the gifted child?

6)   What about the child who is extremely gifted in one area (say art) but close to remedial in another (for instance math)? Should you emphasize his gifted area or his area of difficulty? Like most of us, this child will respond most enthusiastically when receiving strokes for his strength. If you are clever, you can devise ways of drawing his weakest areas into his areas of skill. The scale enlargement of a cartoon or real object could integrate the artistic skills of the forementioned student with his area of numerical difficulty. A poor reader will often wade through materials far beyond him in order to satiate curiosity in his area of talent or interest. Using a child's gifted skills in order to stimulate his weaker areas is a fine solution to the problem.

his weaker areas is a fine solution to the problem.

7)   If you feel inadequate at encouraging the gifted student within the classroom, why not approach the parents about extracurricular enrichment? Many museums or city science centers sponsor special courses, seminars, or programs for elementary students at after school times or on Saturdays. Some parents are not aware of these opportunities, and would be thrilled to enroll their child if they were informed about dates and times. Junior Great Books discussion groups are also timely for some students. As a teacher you should feel qualified to recommend such activities to the appropriate child's parents.

ZERO SELF-CONCEPT

There are numerous ways to apologize. Some people send flowers and chocolates. Others compose sonnets or elegies. Some apologize in the name of peace with honor or $60,000 a year resignations. Then there are those who express their apologies by merely existing; you look at them and immediately sense their fear in erring or failing. They even apologize before the offense by utilizing downcast eyes, indiscernable speech, or jerky, self-conscious movements. It is surprising to discover that many students exhibit the traits of an apologetic person. These students are usually apologetic because they have a low self-concept, or a minimum appreciation for their potential and human worth.

A problem such as the student with zero or low self-concept does not disrupt the classroom routine or cause peer friction. It is one of those silent sleepers that haunt the resources of the teacher. In order to help these students develop their self-concept and self or public image, a quiet, unpresumptive campaign is best staged. As the year progresses and both students and teachers become more familiar, it is easier to support and encourage new patterns of confident behavior.

Possible Solutions

Here are a variety of ways to let the student know her work or self is valued by others:

1)   Use something the child has done as an example of good work. Share it with the class or a small group. Put it up on the wall, or include it in a labelled display. Place work in the hallway or near the entrance to the school. Send the child spontaneously to the principal or the ever-cheery secretary to show off something she has just completed. Choose several students to explain their projects or creations to another class or a younger reading group. Reproduce a child's composition or xerox and distribute it to all the class; use this as a focal for a follow-up assignment or discussion.

2)   Ask the student to do favors for you (such as getting your coat in a rush, opening your wallet for coins, taking messages to other building personnel). Tell the student that you like her to do this because she is so reliable, trustworthy, or whatever the appropriate adjective.

3)   Send bolster notes home extemporaneously when you notice something special about a kid. I have used each Friday as a day when I jot down three to five hand-written notes. These notes I address to both child and parents. I use them only as positive reinforcers, and hand them out inconspicuously right before or during dismissal. Many good feelings develop because of bolster Friday notes. They need not be lengthy.

Sample Bolster Notes

To: Joe and his parents

This is to let you know how pleased I ("we" if a team) am with Joe's sensitivity this week. On several occasions he has made other students feel happier because of his sincere kindness.

Mr. V.

To: Andrea and her parents

This is to let you know how pleased I am with Andrea's progress in learning her multiplication facts. Her eights are glorious!

Ms. V.

4)   Invite the zero concept student to eat lunch with you occasionally. Talk honestly with her about how you have noticed certain nervous habits when she talks before the class. Discuss how she feels during this situation. Talk about a similar problem you once had and how you dealt with it. Support the zero's confidence with lots of compliments and your assurance that she need not worry about her success. Continue this as informally as possible. It's good for the child to verbalize her fears often in hopes of your better understanding them.

DOUBLE TROUBLE

or

The Gruesome Twosome

Best friends are stubborn as graffitti in the bathroom and as synonymous as vacation and peace of mind. Most kids will stick close to their best friends for several months, suddenly face a traumatic mismatch of minds, then laconically join blood forces with a new best friend. Best friends always have best friends, unless they fall into the ostracized scapegoat category.

The best friends problems arise when this combo becomes too exclusive of their peers, too interdependent academically or socially, romantically overinvolved, or highly combustible in combination. The latter explosive reference alludes to the unfortunate truth that some kids get into a lot of trouble together. These problems can be solved, but it will often ruffle the feathers.

Possible Solutions

1) When a certain problem arises that involves the best friends (be it mutual exclusion, interdependence, or acting-out together), you should meet with both of them together to discuss it. You might begin by saying, "I've noticed you two spend a lot of time together. Are you best friends?" Then say, "Have you noticed any certain things that seem to happen when you two are together?" (Yes, we get into trouble a lot or we laugh a lot or we help each other...). Discuss the undesireable behavior. Decide a new behavior, and determine a time when you should meet again to discuss progress. If need be, have the kids write a statement of concern and what they plan to do.

2) If the above proves futile, and given the extra margin of one or two more warnings, then more drastic measures will be necessary. You must specify exact times when the two students may not sit together. Possible times may be lunch time, during films, during music, or during group discussions. Be very strict, but don't outsmart yourself by forbidding them to see one another during times you are absent,

"... AND LET'S NOT TELL ANYONE
WE'RE BEST FRIENDS..."

such as recess or after school. Some students will actually ask you to separate them

at certain times as they admit their weakness in self-discipline when in the company

of their buddy. One student said, "Gol, Ms. V., I just don't know what comes over

me when I'm with John. We have so much fun that I forget what I should be doing, even

if it's something I like to do. We love to goof around, and it always leads to

trouble. I can't help myself and I'm sick of always being in trouble..." When sepa-

rated from his best friend, this boy was very likeable and mildly impish. When with

his friend, he was completely berserk--almost out of touch with reality. He needed the intervention of his teacher and requested it.

3)   Extreme is the case where you forbid two students to interact at all during the day; this is not easily enforced.

4)   Romance can blossom any ol' time. Even grade school fosters the fleet palpatations of romantic infatuation. Depending upon the maturity of the partici- pants, a grade school couple can express affection by such diverse means as kicking and chasing to kissing and petting. On one occasion I have seen a tight, seemingly secure rapport between two fifth graders that was close to adultlike in spirit of communication and depth of mutual caring; however, a case like this is not status quo.

The main problem with grade school romances emerges when a relationship detracts from curricular and social goals. Sometimes a duo may become too heavy for classroom load limits; they may cause undue ruckus and giggling, or become outrage- ously overpublicized and esteemed by their peers. Other times one member of the couple may be too starry eyed or overbearing for the other (who is flattered by the attention but unable to maturely cope with the onslaught).

Interference by the teacher can be dangerous if not properly timed. Before entering in, be certain that your intervention is necessary. Many times, after a month or so, the romance will self-destruct. You could save yourself much entangle- ment by letting social intercourse develop on its own terms. If one of the students complains to you, though, then some advice could be bestowed. Sometimes merely a mention of recent poor work output is a deterrent to rampant flirtations; othertimes calm recognition and acceptance of a duo will be enough to dampen the fires. An example of this occurred once when two students asked to be able to sit with desks close together in my class. I was skeptical so told them that on the next uprooting day they could do just that if they still felt the same. A couple weeks later, they did. However, the constant elbow rubbing seemed overpowering and the two soon dis- solved the partnership. Letting them O.D. on one another was a perfect solution.

Most romances in elementary school are benign, and are best left to the imaginations of the kids. Usually they remain figmented in the imagination, and little action ensues. For those who are more militant, you have twenty or more

years experience to weight against their neophyte flutterings, and usually they are

squelched easily in the classroom by your unstated but omnipotent carnal knowledge.

5)   The physical arrangement of a classroom can solve many double trouble

problems. For specific ideas, refer to Setting the Foundation to Behavior Patterns,

page 11.

THE CLASS SCAPEGOAT

When hot lunches were raised 5¢, it wasn't blamed on inflation. When the

toilets overflowed during parent's visitation, it wasn't the fault of "Dirty Dan the

Dumper". When recesses were cancelled, it wasn't due to the air quality at carbon

monoxide level alert. All of these mishaps were blamed on one person: the class

scapegoat. If by the end of the first two weeks of school there is no one who seems

to fit into the scapegoat role, invisible deliveries of horns, beard, and vulnerable

personnage are arranged. Suddenly one ordinary noontime when Joan's dingdong myster-

iously appears under the derriere of unsuspecting Patty, it was the scapegoat who

put it there. And it's the scapegoat who can hardly answer "yes" or "no" to a ques-

tion, heaven forbid give a straight forward opinion, before she is criticized or

mentally crucified by a majority of her peers. If a Harrison poll were run in class

concerning whether the scapegoat swallowed correctly, indubitabley the results would

indicate 95% feel the scapegoat swallows inappropriately, 4% feel the scapegoat

swallows correctly, and 1% fail to believe the scapegoat actually does swallow. The

scapegoat cannot win. How can kids be so cruel to one another?

At times it is difficult to understand why a particular student is chosen

as class scapegoat. Sometimes it may be by default. But often, it is because the

student has some sort of behavior which consistently irritates the vocal faction of

the class or perhaps encourages teasing by her responses. These vociferous powers

will systematically attack the scapegoat, setting a game-like precedent for the

quieter portion of the class. The trend soon proliferates and becomes status quo.

It is a negative and disasterous problem for the deemed scapegoat, for the class unity, and for the curriculum.

In the hooves of the scapegoat, this is a most painful situation. Oftentimes this student will be chased at recesses or after school, physically and verbally abused, and will suffer much deflation of ego. Each child will deal with the mistreatment in her own manner. Some complain to the teacher, some act as though nothing has happened, some align friends to complain to the teacher, and some actually reform their behavior on their own.

WHO DID IT?

A true pain can transcend when the parents become involved. Too often they do not see the total picture, and feel it is the teacher's fault when the kid gets beat to a pulp on the shortcut home. If the parents had their way, the teacher would become a ubiquitous 24-hour bodyguard, making special arrangements with the secret service to watch the kid while she takes a coffee break. There are, however, those rational parents who are able to sensitively discuss the problem. Working with these parents can be a joy; they can drop you a quick note if here has been a traumatic situation at home or on the way home from school so that you can deal more effectively with the symptoms in the classroom. They will inform you about feedback they receive at home...things about which you may not have heard like the insults traded at the pencil sharpener. Many parents are surprised to learn how their children are relating to their peers, and are as anxious as are you to curb future problems. If you need their help, or they somehow become involved, utilize them as confidantes. Often if the scapegoat knows the parents are communicating with you, she will not be so inclined to attempt to side one faction towards her plight by exaggerating the situation.

What could be done about this problem? The measures for communication in this situation are directed in two areas: toward the scapegoat and toward the remainder of the class.

Possible Solutions for Dealing Directly With:

The Scapegoat

1) The first step is to find out how much the scapegoat is willing to talk about. She knows what is being done to her, but often finds it difficult to verbalize it. As casually as possible, chat one-to-one with the student about how she feels things are going in general or in a particular situation. Perhaps she'll level right away by admitting that the other kids are picking on her. If not, you must continue probing questions that will illicit this observation. You may ask, "How do you think the class (or group) reacted when you gave your ideas this morning? Do

you think this sort of thing happens to you often?" Now, if the student has admitted in any way that there appears to be a problem, then you may go on. If she refuses to recognize the problem then you must continue questioning or else leave the discussion for another time when the problem is more obvious (and painful). No progress can be made until the student firstly admits that a problem exists. Note that no blame is suggested in either direction.

2)   After the problem is defined with the student ("The kids are picking on me"), you may explore possible reasons why this is happening. Begin first with activities the student is doing when negative responses are frequent. Let the student tell you about what happens. Only ask questions such as:

> Can you think of one time when the kids bugged you? Tell me about it.
>
> What did you do to make them act this way?
>
> Were they perhaps reacting to another time when you did something to them?
>
> Tell me about another time.
>
> Do you see any similarities between the first thing you told me about and the second thing you told me about?
>
> What does this tell you?

If you feel that the student is overlooking some distasteful trait about himself (it could even be ring around the collar!) and that he could handle the whole truth, then you should level with him. I like to say, "You know what I've noticed, Scapegoat? I've noticed that you seem to have a tendency to... How does it make you feel when I tell you this?" After this channels should be opened about the student's half of the problem.

3)   The scapegoat will usually try to blame the situation on her peers or rest all hope for alleviation upon the actions of others. Insist that it is a two-way deal, as discussed prior, and say, "You must change your behavior if you want them to change theirs. How can you change your actions so that you won't be made to feel unhappy so often?" Decide upon one thing for the student to do. Keep it simple. Set up a convenient time to check with the student on progress each day, or more often if

necessary. This problem must be dealt with quickly and methodically before it becomes a year-long disruption. When the problem seems less crucial, reestablish a new evaluation time that is less frequent.

Penalties

The peer pressures and abuse tolerated by the scapegoat is ample punishment. There need not be additional penalties. Frequent discussions with the scapegoat seem most helpful; honesty about how the scapegoat relates is usually best. Be very complimentary when the scapegoat handles a situation tactfully; reinforce her immediately in a private way, but at the same time let her know when and if she is off base.

Possible Solutions for Dealing With:

The Class in Regards to the Scapegoat

1) Whether or not you approach the class about this problem or counsel with isolated factions within the class depends upon how you view the situation or how advanced or proliferated it is. If you feel the scapegoat will be able to eliminate the conflict by augmenting her own behavior, then there is no need to involve the peer group. If, however, the situation demands behavior change by members of the class, then you must approach the peer group.

2) Approaching the scapegoat's peers may be done with or without the scapegoat present. You must judge which media would be most appropriate. I prefer to deal with these sorts of problems early in the morning during our usual rap sessions. There are several ways to handle the format:

a) You may choose to keep things casual by introducing the topic impersonally by role playing or by asking, "What would you guys do if your best friend were always being picked-on by other kids?" Sometimes a general talk such as this is enough to get the point across without mentioning that it is occurring within the class. Kids, being startlingly up front, will often see your point immediately and not hesitate to point out problems within the class. This may be the healthiest, most natural way to air grief and pent-up hostilities.

b) Other times you may choose to indicate that the problem to be discussed is one found in this class: "We have a problem in this class. I've noticed it is becoming disruptive during many activities, so I think we should talk about it. The problem is that a certain person is being picked on. Let's not use any names today. We will just start by describing some times when we have been the victim ourselves, or times when we have seen other kids being victimized and how it made us feel at that time." After feeling out the kids' empathy level, the problem could become more specific. Sometimes even when dealing with the specific problem, it is easier for the kids to discuss it rationally if they don't use names; the tendency is to be less accusative, vindictive or defensive when names are not stressed.

c) Or you may choose to use a format similar to (b), but use the child's name. During this situation the scapegoat could be present or not. Sometimes it is good to privately tell the scapegoat that you are going to discuss the problem at the class meeting and to ask whether or not she would like to be there and whether or not you should use real names.

3) Important, no matter which format you use, is procuring a commitment from the class members about their behavior. Be sure to have a class member sum up the discussion, and restate the workable solution. Designate a time soon in the future to evaluate progress. The atmosphere in approaching the problem should be positive, a feeling of mutual helping in order to make the classroom a happier, more congenial place.

Penalties

After counseling such as the above, if certain individuals persist in antagonizing the student, you may restrict their privileges, regulate their exposure to the scapegoat (try not to schedule them in the same small group situations), or contact the parents for a conference. Seldom will these steps be necessary if the scapegoat problem is recognized and tackled in the early stages.

THE LAZY ONE

This student definitely isn't the one who makes you wake up screaming in the night; she only causes you to flacidly pull out your hairs one-by-one as you go over incoming assignments. Most often this student is bright, and capable of high-standard output. I find the lazy student usually to have a creative twist, and more times than not, she recognizes the phony value of busy work or tedium and is wise for only half-doing it. However, there are times when the lazy student must be pushed by you in order to maximize her capabilities. Depending upon this student's potential and your feelings about the importance of busy work, daily work,

and content quality, you may or may not feel the need to try a few tricks.

Possible Solutions

1)   If you feel the lazy student's work to be substandard, it is best to confront the student honestly about your feelings. Leaving it open like this (as your feeling, or opinion) the student also will often volunteer her opinion, and then volunteer to redo the work. If the student does not agree with you, then you may choose to agree with the student for perhaps she is right, or you may further discuss why you believe it important to produce work of higher quality. At this point you may either wait for the student to volunteer to redo it, let it go with a warning about future quality, or reassign the work.

Watch out for a sudden great improvement in quality for a five day period followed by a gradual relapse. It is helpful to reinforce the student frequently when her work shows depth. A follow-up conference is wise, too. Many times I prefer to arrange a follow-up conference for six to ten days past the first confrontation. This gives the student a chance to work to a given date, receive feedback, and to take it from there according to revised goals.

2)   Suppose you tried the above, but the work has not improved. This is no fun. You could talk with the student again, but perhaps it is time to pose a deadly threat. The threat, of course, depends upon the student. I personally feel that it is not advantageous to penalize a student by taking away other curricular activities she enjoys (such as P.E., art, or music) because these are important parts of the curriculum just like math or reading, or to penalize a student by making a task more gruesome or laborious. This is not positive, and only makes for hard feelings. We're in the Ed Biz because we like to see kids excited, and we do not want to turn them off too early. Hopefully they will learn about life from the natural consequences of their actions, not because of some forced educational threat. If you feel this way, there isn't a lot more that you can do to maximize the student's output if she is not interested, either. However, the old slap of accountability is

86

still a stinging reality; if the teacher does not make the kid produce, who will? So says the public. In some hard core cases, you may find it necessary to impose ridiculous threats to the student. Hopefully these will accomplish the goal of "forcing her to learn" rather than turning her off totally to school and to you. Before taking this extreme step, it is best to find out how the parents feel. If they are of the laissez-faire vintage, then it is logical to also assume that posture. Trying to force a student to do work at school when the parents offer no support is an uphill battle. Usually the outcome of such a situation is a hostile child and associated learning difficulties. You may still encourage the student to perform at a standard deemed appropriate, but you need not go bald on a crusade that will not be enforced at home. If, however, the parents feel it important to raise performance standards, then you should seek an opinion and a commitment from them on how you could work together with their child on this problem. It is usually best to meet first with parents or phone them for "climate trial", then have a conference or decision making session that includes the child.

It is horrendously exciting to work through the home on a child's problem. Often when talking with parents, it is evident that the lazy trend carries over into the home environment through housework or home obligations. When the student realizes that teacher and parents are unified and communicating, she will usually pull in her horns and buckle down.

Penalties

1)   The lazy student is not a class disrupter, but one of those who methodically drips away at the back of the conscience, eroding all those fantasies of successful teaching. As discussed previously, penalties with the lazy student can be more hassle than it's worth. If you feel the necessity to force the student to achieve, then the brutal sentence of redoing every substandard assignment may be imposed. This is difficult to enforce because it necessitates regradeing papers, following up on the second drafting, and remembering to chase after those second-run jobs. How-

ever, if you are religious about your penalty, it can bring about fast results. Hopefully you will not kill the joy of learning.

2)   When assignments seem to be left at home ("Oh, I guess I forgot it...") everyday, have the kid call home to make sure someone is there, then require her to <u>walk</u> (Mom may <u>not</u> bring the work by car) and retreive it, making up missed class time after school. Following about one session on the road, the lazy one usually has to find another alibi.

3)   There is also the penalty of lower evaluative marks or less positive re-inforcement. This hasn't worked for a few hundred years, so why do we use it?

THE SUPERIOR SNOB

After just so many years of being one of the most brilliant and enlightened students to excel through the system, school inevitably becomes tedious and mundane. The superior snob speciman, after putting up with the mindless masses too long, then drops out. This turgid personality usually refrains from joining into the spirit of the classroom, interacts with her inferiors as little as possible, and makes little attempt to mask impatience or scoffing in regards to the performance of her peers. She may act indifferent to everyone, except maybe a few who she feels merit the recog-nition of intelligence.

This kid oftentimes <u>is</u> superior to her peers in all areas except humility and compassion. Depending upon the purpose of education in your professional repertoire or whether you emphasize cognitive or affective traits, the student may or may not have a problem in your classroom. She would in mine.

My hope for the superior snob would be to deepen her social conscience, increase her peer empathy, and to help her to be a kid and hang out for the year--- at least while she's at school. This problem may be one to approach hopefully, but to let go if not disruptive to the class. After all, it is the kid's right to remain to herself. Just because she does not put up a big social front it does not mean she is destructive to the class, although her antisocial behavior could possibly convert into a disruptive form. What's really important is: Is she happy that way? If so, leave her in peace. If not, (as you see it) try a few ideas. When they are unsuccessful, perhaps it would be best to leave and let be...

Possible Solutions

1)   Through group discussions, try to drive home the point that each person is of value to humanity for her own personnage or her unique characteristics. An excellent way to convey this is to utilize the famous (and hopefully not too overused) role playing situation of choosing ten people to survive a nuclear holocaust from a list of twenty personality types and professions. Or discuss which three qualities the kids feel are most valuable in human beings (for example, kindness, sincerety, intelligence, etc.). There are a variety of techniques suitable to your particular classroom situation, be it dramatic role playing, small group discussions, or large group talks.

2)   If the snob shows potential for compassion, ask her to tutor a slow child in another classroom; many times she will be sympathetic to a child who is not in her chronological division.

3)   Directly approach the snob; discuss how she feels about other kids and offer your support. Since the problem may not disturb anyone except the student herself (and perhaps you are wrong there, too) and your image of what the well-rounded

grammar school personality should be, then this may be the point to leave off.

Penalties

Unless the student is overly obnoxious (putting down other kids for their inadequacies or mistakes), no penalties need be imposed. Usually a sharp retort in private or a well-aimed "look" will do the trick.

THE SMELLY ONE

Forbidden Fragrance

School designers have a repressed fear of fresh air, stocking faith in the dusty fan or ventilation system. Meanwhile, twenty-five hot and heaving kids are stacked and stuffed into a seemingly spacious floor area (at least it looked great on the plans...but we forgot to include pictures of each desk, each chair, and each child hovering over the chair...not to mention coats, lunches, gym clothes and the four thousand latest 3-D art projects all simultaneously conceived). After a steamy late spring recess when infinite separate and desperate slurps have dripped back from the water fountain and countless beads of fifth grade sweat have met at the eyebrows, you are aware of a strange, haunting odor. The first day it merely hints at the problem. You hope it is only Jenny's tuna and banana sandwich. But, the second hot day of spring, during a quiet time of desk work, you are positive that this odor is not plant or mineral, but humanoid. By strolling nonchalantly around it is easy to determine the source. You try not to faint openly. What's to be done?

The first time this happened in my class I recalled back when I was a sixth grader: there was a girl two rows over who smelled like three week old urine-soaked bedding. It was a nightmare for us, and no one did anything about it. I used to have hateful fantasies about ducking her into ten vats of Mr. Clean or burning that smelly, pink, stained satin dress she wore on the most intense days. So I vowed that when I grew up and was a teacher I would never force my class to endure such olfactory torture. Remembering this now as a real teacher, in one particular case I spoke to a student offender privately, telling her that I noticed an unpleasant odor when around her, and that she was at an age when many bodily changes occur, and that perhaps it would be necessary to bathe more frequently and/or use deodorant. We had a very informative discussion and I congratulated myself upon saving my class from the second generation of the pink satin nightmare. Only to be awarded the next day with a parental-principal conference featuring two extremely irate parents who believed I had told their daughter she stank ('tis true), to wear a bra (not true), and use deodorant (only suggested it), etc., etc. "...and we're not an unclean family because we buy deodorant by the case when it's on sale at Piggly Wiggly..." The audacity! It was, indeed, Pink Satin Revisited. What a conference! But in the end, our nostrils were all happier and I believe it was worth an uncomfortable confrontation. I never figured out how the bra got into it, but deduced that the girl wanted to wear one and felt it was a great opportunity to get Mom and Dad to buy one when

required by the teacher.

Possible Solutions

Suggestions for solving the problem without Pink Satin Hallucinations:

1)   Try talking to the whole class about cleanliness. Do a couple mini lessons on it for a week. Charts are a good way ("How Many Times I Brushed My Left Molar Last Week"). Talk about grooming, hair care, skin care, sweat glands, and maybe invite a dermatologist or beauty specialist to the class. My sister had a teacher who used to put on deodorant everyday before lunch in front of the class to demonstrate the importance of such non-offensive contact. This could be getting carried away.

2)   If the group hygiene approach is sudsless, you are compelled to hold a private conference. It is best to be straight to the point, because it is embarrassing to tell someone they stink no matter how nice you may be. Include several ways of eliminating the problem: changing underclothers daily, washing daily (and where to do it!), and possibly using deodorant. Point out that it is difficult for others to study and learn when such an unpleasant environment surrounds them. Hopefully the student can handle this on her own.

3)   If necessary, a conference with parents could be your next step. For this, it might be handy to include the nurse or counselor as well as the student.

4)   If all else fails, why not make gas masks for a science project?

THE HOSTILE ONE

Soggy grape gum under the desk, two month-old macaroni and cheese lunches and dirty P.E. socks, all those things are part of a day. But one thing you don't need: that negative creep over there by the ventilator with the "I've got you smile" on her face. She could drive you mad. What's more, she is super smart, super talented, and right-on as far as most of her methods of driving you mad (or causing you to break the lead on your new NEA red pencil). That wise cheshire cat!

The hostile student does not endear herself to you, and is a powerful lobbyist among other students of like inclination. If the negative, hostile student is not dealt with early she becomes the sinister leader of a most evil force. Usually her efforts are in protest of the teacher's authority, school as an institution, or against some objectionable faction of her peers. The reason she is so threatening is because she is usually intelligent, a leader, and able to psychologically outmaneuver you if unchecked. It is not much fun to teach in this situation.

The overuse of foul language is a problem not necessarily associated with hostile kids, but their negative feelings often foster its use. Your particular tolerance of casual swearing as opposed to derogatory foul language will be governed by your personal values as well as those of the community in which your school is located. Lots of kids will swear just to be mellow. A large urban school situation in the East may culturally condone the mundane usage of many four letter words which would boggle the mind of an elementary school westerner.

Personal disdain for the hostile student is often inevitable. However, it is essential never to show your dislike of this student's personality or let her know that her name causes instant mental nausea. You may show your dislike for her behavior, though. Usually this malign student will already know how to hurt or anger you, but the less emotion you exhibit to her, the less reinforcement she receives.

Possible Solutions

Here are some possible ways of habitating the same negative educational body space with the hostile student:

1)   I could tell you about all the weary, self-annihilating hours I've spent dealing with hostile students, attempting to outmaneuver them or analyzing my past blunders. But it's too painful. In the past I've tried being passive, compassionate, giving, loving, forgiving. But now, when I see a hostile student, I don the stiff upper lip and the "no nonsense" aura. I say, "We do not act that way in this class." I will not tolerate it. Period. Mostly, I am forced to do this because I am overly sensitive and tend to personalize too many incidents. Thus, to protect myself from being hurt, I try to prevent a hostile student from affronting me early. Other

teachers may be able to cope with the hostile student less militantly. I am more reactionary because of my vulnerability in this area.

First off a private discussion is the favorite remedy. Talking with the hostile student is like conversing with a mute wolverine; when the silence is broken, it's usually fierce, gnashing, destructive, invectives that are aired. Providing the appropriate atmosphere for these strong feelings to be released is the primary problem. The hostile student is usually so totally turned off that she will refuse to cooperate, even though she has many deep feelings that she would like or needs to express. Try to establish an atmosphere that is nonthreatening to enable the negative student to open up. If she is immediately put on the defensive, she will refuse to cooperate in the least. A good way to open the conversation is to say,

WHOEVER SAID TWO NEGATIVES EQUAL A POSITIVE

"Hostile One, how have you been feeling about yourself lately?" Too heavy? Or "How do you like what we've been doing at school?" Too blah? Or, "Your art work yesterday was dynamite. How did you get that idea?" Too goody two shoes? Then design your own opening. While the student is able to rap about positive feelings, she may bring up an idea that has been bothering her. If the chat thus far has been positive and open, it's a good sign that delving into more sensitive areas could be initiated. Allow the student to explain her view before expressing your own. This discussion should include your personal reactions to the student's behavior as well as the class's reactions, with the outcome being a commitment by the student to change her negative behavior. A signed statement composed by the student is the best insurance of sincerity. At this point, tell the student that if a change is not evident by a certain date, her parents will be called for a conference. Stripping of school honors (like student government) is also a threat. Any threats should be reasonable so that they could actually be enforced. Meet again with the student periodically to check progress.

Don't be shocked if after a week or two a lapse of behavior occurs. This is common, and a fresh start should begin. A preventative measure for this would be lots of feedback in the form of notes home (see page 73, Zero Self-Concept) or quick student conferences. The student should be made to see that her behavior is noticed, and that any positive changes are appreciated by you, her fellow students, and other school personnel.

2)   If the road to progress seems perilous and disconcerting, a conference with parents is the next best step. Whether you choose to have the student attend the conference from the beginning would depend upon the situation. I often prefer to speak first with the parents, then have the student in to explain her role and set a goal. Be sure to notice the interractions of parents and child; this will oftentimes explain a child's behavior. Many times a hostile child will have an extremely strict father or mother who rides hard on her at home. This leaves school as an outlet for frustrations felt at home, or as a demonstration sight for bad feelings about

95

authoritarian figures. If the school does not impose the same heavy hand as father or mother, it will not be as effective, being that the child is regulated at home by "the hand". The most obnoxious monster in class is often transformed to a docile, humble peon in the presence of a parent conference. Thus, with the aid of parents, a child can often become better behaved at school. Just the thought of parents hearing about the weird things the hostile kid does at school embarrasses or unfortunately frightens her. It is humiliating for the child when Dad and Mom find out the negative way she has been acting. Now granted, this method of control is not the greatest for nurturing a well-adjusted and happy child in the classroom---it is close to suppression. But it is not the first alternative that you would try either. Try other positive ways first.

Most important, you cannot let a negative child destructively run your class at all or you have lost for the year; she will refrigerate your class ambience like a relentless minstrel. If she responds to none of your positive treatment readily, do not waste time with roses, lollipops and slobbery smiles. Put on the straight face, call the parents, and end that chicanery. Do not allow the child to even look negative in class. If the child feels she can control you, it is curtains and year-end inventories for you. You must never give in at the beginning with this dangerous problem. Don't even let a smirk get by. Once you are even-steven with the student, after a few painful days of 1984 Big Brothering and never turning your back, the student will get the idea that you are more stubborn than she, and that should do it. It is such a bothersome, petty thing to go through, but it will pay off in the long run when you are not forced to contend with a pack of hostile students who have followed the negative lead of one vociferous organizer.

3)   If you feel the need to curtail the extent of foul language usage in your classroom or with the hostile child, it is best to be consistent about it from the first day.

When dealing with the class as a whole, most often you are faced with rather benign four letter words used in kids' writing. Certain expressions may get

96

by in the literary sense. However, if you notice one student (or a trend for several students) to be obsessed in the use of such expressions, you might say, "Using language such as that is okay in your own home if your parents permit it or if you have decided it is a good way for you to speak. However, at school we must associate with lots of kinds of people, many who are offended by swearing. Therefore we will not use this sort of language in our writing or speaking at school. It is a way to show respect to our friends here, even if we believe differently than do they."

When dealing privately with the four letter offender, the same logic as used with the whole class may be employed. If this does not sink in, you may be obliged to have the child write down her foul language and send it home to her parents along with an explanatory note or phone call from you. This usually puts a screeching halt to the problem.

4)   Last resort (after parent conference): Consult the principal and/or guidance counselor. Work out something there. This is not a penalty for the child; it is a method whereby a problem may be solved. Do not use the principal or counselor as a threat. She or he is there to give you insight, a little weight, and to relieve your burden by helping you and the student cope with the situation.

Penalties

1)   The hostile student is often a leader who holds a coveted position of leadership in the school (student council, patrol, lunch deliveries). Use your executive privilege of veto to impose the possibility of impeachment or removal. Give the student a certain time period of probation from the activity, complete with an official probation form:

```
        Date _____

_____(name)_____    is on probation from _(position)_

_____because of _____

_____.  This behavior must be termin-

ated by ____(date)_____ .  A meeting will be held on the

above date to judge whether or not the behavior has improved.

        Signed,

                    _____ student

                    _____ teacher

                    _____ parent
```

Right away tell the kid that you're not accustomed to having school leaders acting

that way, and that you will see to it personally that she does not keep her office

unless her behavior changes. Tell her that as a school officer she should be setting

an example (the ol' one-two routine).

2)   Ask the child to write down her recent disturbing behavior. Have her also

write down what she could have done differently and how she should do it the next

time a similar situation arises. Send it home to be signed by parents.

3)   If the situation is a serious one, do not allow the child to make decisions

as do her classmates. For example, you may delegate where she sits, assign her to

small group activities rather than permitting her to choose a group, require a cer-

tain activity during unstructured times. Explain to her, "I am telling you to do this

rather than letting you choose because your behavior today has shown me that you do

not make wise decisions for yourself. You will be able to choose when you show me

that you are responsible for your decisions."

4)   If the student is complaining about a certain assignment or duty, you may

choose to assign her more. And more each time she complains. As mentioned in the discussion of the Lazy One, this penalty does not add to the joy of learning and will possibly be deleterious to your real purpose in teaching. Using such a negative penalty as this is definitely a last choice.

5)   Assign the book Pollyanna to be read and reported upon.

THE FAT KID

or

Complications of the Big Mac

Did you ever wish that you hadn't packed two Big Macs in your rucksac on the bus during rush hour? Mashed between the masses of starving, rung-out frazzles of the business world and the famished, dowdy department store bargain seekers, that fast-food aroma sneaks out of the sterile white sack like a Biafran Nightmare. People on the bus wonder how rapid transit was able to arrange a MacDonalds franchise during an economic recession, moreover, a franchise between 59th and 125th streets! You repeatedly catch drifting wasps of that warm, greasy smell, and cannot determine whether it is nauseating or comforting. It reminds you that you are hungry, but simultaneously asks why you are about to eat such a concoction. Suddenly you envision your cheeks coated with Big Mac guke and your arms puffing out like pale bratwursts. You could actually be mistaken for that gastronmical catastrophe: THE FAT KID!

The fat kid strikes American classrooms each year. Sometimes she even comes in second helpings. It is a condition perpetuated by smuggled Mars Bars, subversive twinkies, and vicariously disguised fast foods (such as the potato chip disguised as Adele Davis). How can kids get fat so young when it took us teachers years? Why is it such an American phenomena?

Everyone loves it when the fat kid sits on a tack, or when she has to get weighed by the room mothers in front of the whole class on health day. Such are the joys of elementary terrorist activities. If there are no minority students worth victimizing, then at least there's always the fat kid.

Cutting the Big Mac down to Baby Burger:

1)   Do not allow the other classmembers to make fun of the fat kid. If need be, talk privately with those who are offensive. Stress during class meetings the importance of appreciating people for their good qualities, rather than emphasizing their peculiarities. Some time after a particularly good discussion about put-down statements, have everyone in the circle point out one good quality about the person to their right. Repeat this several times during the year to reinforce the aware-ness of peers' individual characteristics.

2)   Have a nutrition unit. Study food groups. Let students record their food intake for a week, compose menus for the hot lunch program, plan menus for their

THE LIVING EXAMPLE

family with Mom and Dad, and talk tons about Big Macdom.

3)   Encourage the fat student in gym. Do not let her out of exercises, nor cease to encourage her. Ask her to run errands for you quickly. Keep her doing active things. Have the fat kid help the P.E. specialist with one or two younger classes weekly. Often times whereas she is inhibited at jiggling her flab in front of her own peers, she will readily shake it when setting an example for and working with younger students.

4)   Talk with the parents to discover their viewpoint of the situation. Many parents are concerned, but have not yet realized how seriously impeded is their youngster by her obesity. Other parents are informed but frustrated. Determining a possible course of action which will be reinforced both at home and at school is possible when working with the parents. Suggesting medical or nutritional referral is timely; many parents may not realize the importance of obesity to their child's social and physical health.

5)   Nagging about the problem is not appropriate. However, if the student realizes that you are aware of her problem and that you are concerned, it may give her an extra ounce of willpower. Engage the student in a private conversation if you feel comfortable about it, and encourage her to set reasonable weekly nutritional goals.

Sometimes you may be tempted to jump whole hog into the reformation of the fat kid. But remember that there are but six hours times five days weekly that you will influence the fat kid; the rest of the 18 hours daily are spent under home supervision. Being that the child's problems of weight control probably originated at home, you have little control over the situation outside the classroom. Your job as a teacher is not to regulate the child's nutritional fortitude. Let the parents or physician handle it. You may definitely work with the parents as part of a dietary program, but certainly it is unreasonable to think you could radically change the situation in your six hours at school.

THE PERFECT KID

The Utopian Dream Alias The Kool Whip Trip

Everytime you look in his direction you think, "Wow, what a delight!"
He's smart (but not too smart), sensitive (but not overly so), alert, coordinated,
sincere, creative, artistic, scientific, poised, a leader, a good group member,
musical, responsible.

There seems no justification for worrying about the perfect kid and his
impeccable personnage, until you notice those telltale signs: visible unrest in
discussions, boredom during written work, lack of puns or hilarious cynical remarks
(always tasteful, of course), tendencies to act out with other negative forces,
disinterest or general lethargy from all points of view (he even gave away three of
his 200 Boy Scout merit badges at lunchtime!). Is the perfect kid really a problem?
In the back of your conscience lurks a deep dark "yes", but out front you are too
busy deterring the escalation of other rampant social ills to do anything about it.

What causes apathetic behaviors in the perfect kid? Usually, the perfect
kid is merely going through a phase; the behavior may be due to many factors: family,
school, peers, or other. At times it may be due to lack of attention on the part of
the teacher. While wrestling with the alligators, don't forget to cuddle the lamb
from time to time.

Another unsettling problem with the perfect kid is that he is so obsequi-
ously perfect it makes you wonder whether or not something is getting past you, or
that why are you there because you are not doing anything for the kid, or that is
he normal because he never goofs off, or that is he paid off by the mafia to totally
disengorge the teacher's inborn will to reform? If this perfection of studentdom
always likely to provoke the apathy discussed in the prior paragraph? Probably not.
Some perfect kids just keep being pneumatically perfect no matter what---they even
goof off the perfect amount---and there is not much you can do about it.

When evaluation time rolls around, the perfect kid presents yet another
problem to the teacher: What can you write on his conference report? It is often-

times difficult to set challenging yet reasonable goals for the perfect kid when his work is already so great. After writing so many complimentary descriptions of the perfect kid's output, it becomes a bit overbearing. The perfect kid needs constructive criticism just like his peers.

Possible Solutions

Here is what to do to keep stimulating that perfect kid:

1)   Be aware of the perfect kid; make sure you reinforce, challenge and encourage him in many quiet ways. He is perceptive and lively, thus you need only direct his enthusiasm from time to time or rekindle his spirit. Send a few high brow puns his way when addressing the class. It may fly over the masses, but the perfect kid will get it and love it.

2)   Beware of having the perfect kid as your golden nugget. Always asking him to help you or do special things will alienate him from the rest of the class. Don't let your admiration or fondness for the perfect kid become obvious.

3)   In evaluating the perfect kid, don't let his charisma and charm overwhelm you. Try to set a reasonable goal for him to attain (such as, "George should strive to make a mistake now and then..."). Choose an area for development that will strengthen the child's weakest skills. Actively engage the student in improving this area so that he feels involved in a self-oriented goal.

NAME: Perfect Kid REPORT CARD	SUPERIOR	GOOD	FAIR	NEEDS IMPROVEMENT
ARITHMETIC	✓			
READING	✓			
YOGA	✓			
LEADERSHIP	✓			
COOPERATION	✓			
"Mistake making"				✓

DEBRIEFING AND DESENSITIZATION: BACKWARD

As you cram that last dissheveled file into the cardboard box where you will store it during the summer months until next fall when you have so much more time to be organized, and as you close the classroom door for the final time in June, you marvel at how you managed to scramble through another year; how you leaped from the first orientation to Halloween and before you knew it, spring reports were due. All of that among thousands of disarming and hilarious anecdotes. You are alternately swept with varying waves of remorse over things you never accomplished, with guilt about the time you spoke too sharply to quiet Ben, and with warmth for the morning when Sean cried as he told you about his dog getting run over, while at the same time your feet are automatically scurrying savagely to escape this chalky, neonlit, four-walled mad house. At last, peace and quiet. Limp and washed-out, you wonder why you come back to it each year. What a relief to get out of there. You will go home, put your feet up, have a cool, frothy beer, and do nothing.

While you are relaxing and doing nothing maybe you will be able to think of some ideas for next year, and won't it be fun to contrive all those wild, enticing new adventures? You can hardly wait!